THE EASY CHRISTMAS SON

K

Melody, Lyrics and Simplifie

M000168573

Over 100 Songs THE in the Key of "C"

THE
EASY
CHRISTMAS
SONGS
FAKE
BOOK

ISBN 978-1-5400-2911-9

Visit Hal Leonard Online at
www.halleonard.com

Contact Us:
Hal Leonard
7777 West Bluemound Road
Milwaukee, WI 53213
Email: info@halleonard.com

In Europe contact:
Hal Leonard Europe Limited
Distribution Centre, Newmarket Road
Bury St Edmunds, Suffolk, IP33 3YB
Email: info@halleonardeurope.com

In Australia contact:
Hal Leonard Australia Pty. Ltd.
4 Lentara Court
Cheltenham, Victoria, 3192 Australia
Email: info@halleonard.com.au

THE EASY CHRISTMAS SONGS FAKE BOOK

CONTENTS

INTRODUCTION

What Is a Fake Book?

A fake book has one-line music notation consisting of melody, lyrics and chord symbols. This lead sheet format is a "musical shorthand" which is an invaluable resource for all musicians—hobbyists to professionals.

Here's how *The Easy Christmas Songs Fake Book* differs from most standard fake books:

- All songs are in the key of C.

- Many of the melodies have been simplified.

- Only five basic chord types are used—major, minor, seventh, diminished and augmented.

- The music notation is larger for ease of reading.

In the event that you haven't used chord symbols to create accompaniment, or your experience is limited, a chord speller chart is included at the back of the book to help you get started.

Have fun!

ALL I WANT FOR CHRISTMAS IS YOU

Words and Music by MARIAH CAREY
and WALTER AFANASIEFF

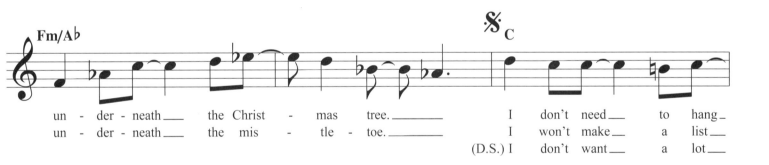

- mas day.___ I just want you for ___ my own,___
- deer click.___ I just want you here ___ to - night,___
___ my door.___ I just want him for ___ my own,___

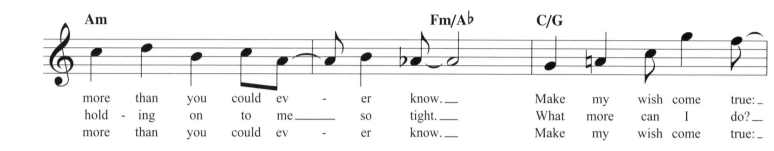

more than you could ev - er know.___ Make my wish come true:_
hold - ing on to me ___ so tight.___ What more can I do?_
more than you could ev - er know.___ Make my wish come true:_

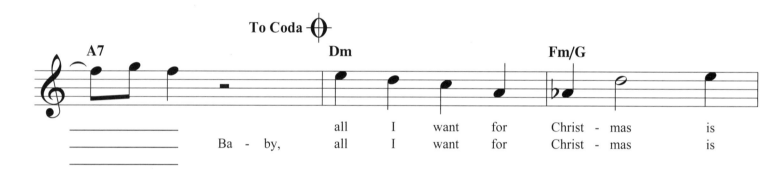

___ all I want for Christ - mas is
___ Ba - by, all I want for Christ - mas is

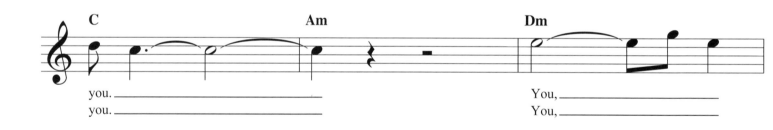

you._____ You,_____
you._____ You,_____

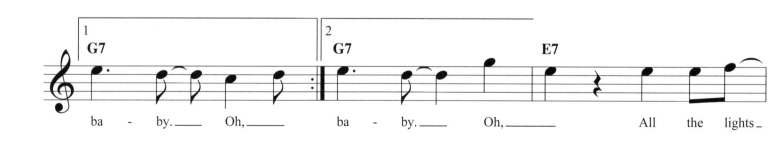

ba - by.___ Oh,___ ba - by.___ Oh,_____ All the lights_

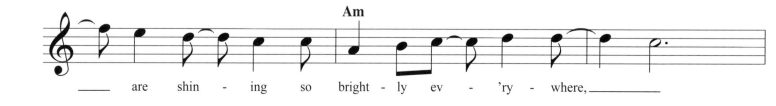

___ are shin - ing so bright - ly ev - 'ry - where,_____

and the sound___ of chil - dren's laugh - ter fills___ the air. __

___ And ev - 'ry - one___ is sing - ing,

I hear those sleigh___ bells ring - ing. San - ta, won't you please bring me

what I real - ly need? Won't you please bring my ba - by to me?___ Oh, __

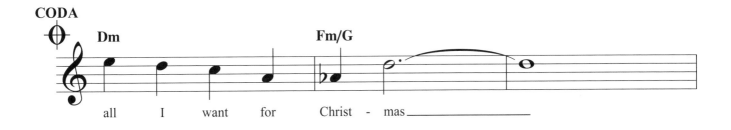

all I want for Christ - mas___

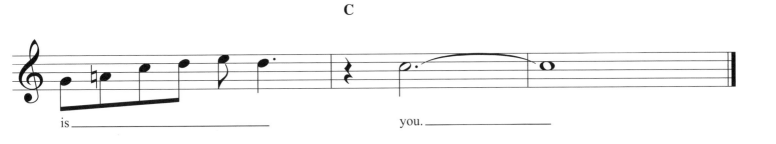

is ___ you. ___

ALL I WANT FOR CHRISTMAS IS MY TWO FRONT TEETH

Words and Music by
DON GARDNER

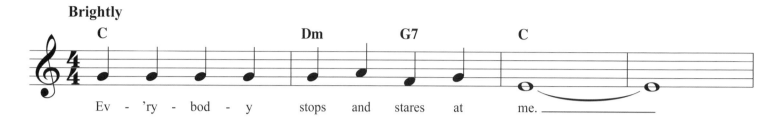

Brightly

Ev - 'ry - bod - y stops and stares at me. ____

These two teeth are gone as you can see. ____

I don't know just who to blame for this ca - tas - tro - phe, but

my one wish on Christ - mas Eve is as plain as it can be!

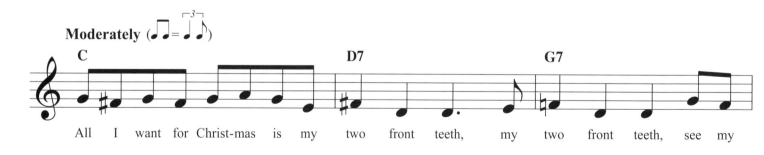

Moderately

All I want for Christ-mas is my two front teeth, my two front teeth, see my

two front teeth. Gee, if I could on - ly have my two front teeth, then

I could wish you "Mer - ry Christ - mas!" It

seems so long since I could say, "Sis - ter Su - sie sit - ting on a

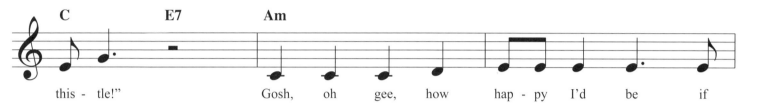

this - tle!" Gosh, oh gee, how hap - py I'd be if

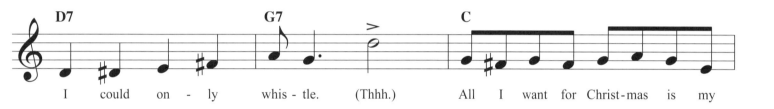

I could on - ly whis - tle. (Thhh.) All I want for Christ-mas is my

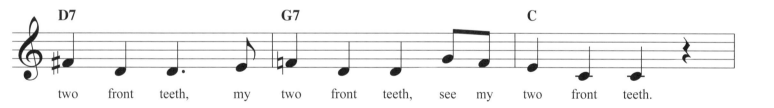

two front teeth, my two front teeth, see my two front teeth.

Gee, if I could on - ly have my two front teeth, then

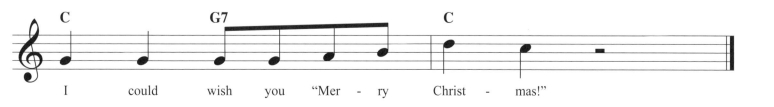

I could wish you "Mer - ry Christ - mas!"

AS LONG AS THERE'S CHRISTMAS
from BEAUTY AND THE BEAST - THE ENCHANTED CHRISTMAS

Music by RACHEL PORTMAN
Lyrics by DON BLACK

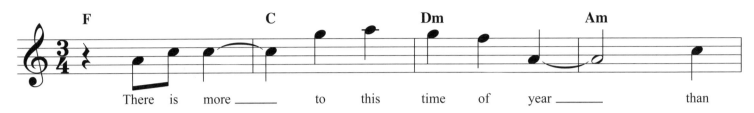

There is more _____ to this time of year _____ than

sleigh _ bells and hol - ly, mis - tle - toe and snow. These things will come and

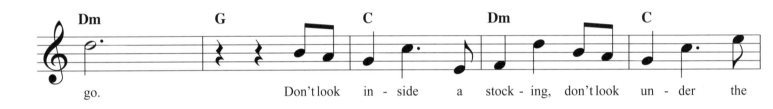

go. Don't look in - side a stock - ing, don't look un - der the

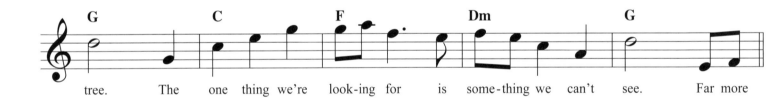

tree. The one thing we're look-ing for is some-thing we can't see. Far more

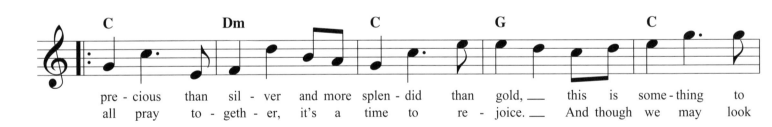

pre - cious than sil - ver and more splen - did than gold, _ this is some - thing to
all pray to - geth - er, it's a time to re - joice. _ And though we may look

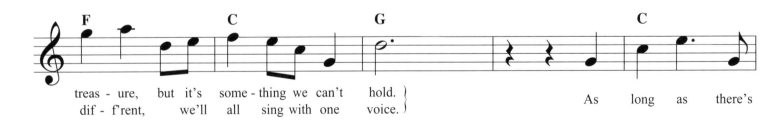

treas - ure, but it's some - thing we can't hold. }
dif - f'rent, we'll all sing with one voice. }   As long as there's

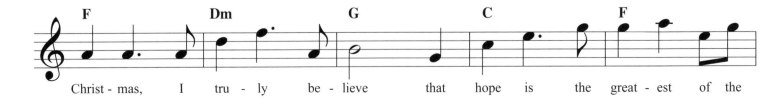

Christ - mas, I tru - ly be - lieve that hope is the great - est of the

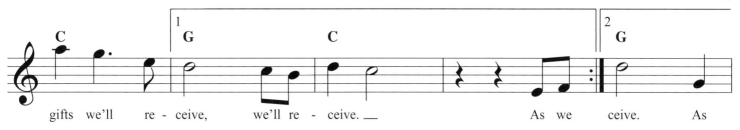

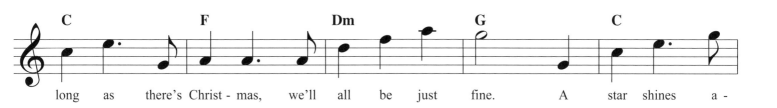

gifts we'll re - ceive, we'll re - ceive. ___ As we ceive. As

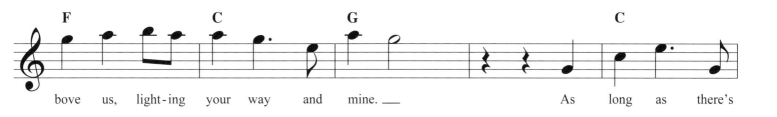

long as there's Christ - mas, we'll all be just fine. A star shines a -

bove us, light - ing your way and mine. ___ As long as there's

Christ - mas I tru - ly be - lieve that hope is the great - est of the

gifts we'll re - ceive. As long as our guid - ing star ___ shines a -

bove, ___ there'll al - ways be Christ - mas, ___ so there al - ways will

be a time ___ when the world is filled with peace and love. ___

BABY, IT'S COLD OUTSIDE
from the Motion Picture NEPTUNE'S DAUGHTER

By FRANK LOESSER

I real - ly can't stay, _____ I've got to go 'way. _____
sim - ply must go, _____ the an - swer is No! _____

_____ This eve - ning has been _____ so ver - y nice. _____
_____ The wel - come has been _____ so nice and warm. _____

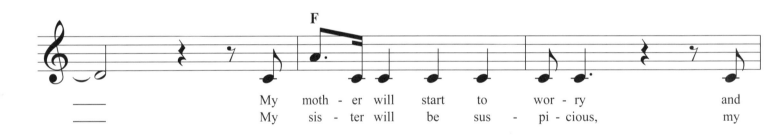

_____ My moth - er will start to wor - ry and
_____ My sis - ter will be sus - pi - cious, my

fa - ther will be pac - ing the floor. So real - ly I'd bet - ter
broth - er will be there at the door. My maid - en aunt's mind is

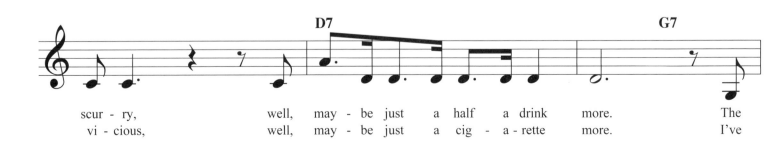

scur - ry, well, may - be just a half a drink more. The
vi - cious, well, may - be just a cig - a - rette more. I've

neigh - bors might think; _____ say, what's in this drink? _____
got to get home; _____ say, lend me a comb. _____

_____ I wish I knew how _____ to break the
_____ You've real - ly been grand, _____ but don't you

spell. _____ I ought to say "No, no,
see? _____ There's bound to be talk to -

no, sir!" At least I'm gon - na say that I tried. I
mor - row. At least there will be plen - ty im - plied. I

real - ly can't stay, _____ ah, but it's cold _____ out -
real - ly can't stay, _____ ah, but it's cold _____ out -

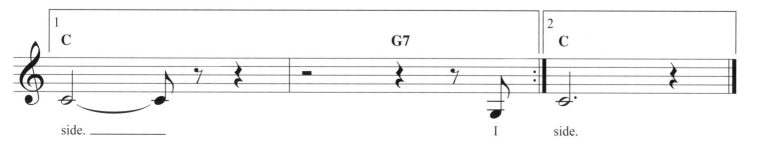

side. _____ I side.

BECAUSE IT'S CHRISTMAS
(For All the Children)

Music by BARRY MANILOW
Lyric by BRUCE SUSSMAN and JACK FELDMAN

Moderately

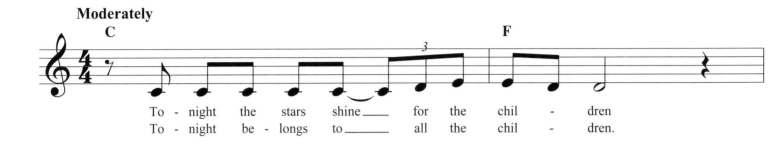

To - night the stars shine____ for the chil - dren
To - night be - longs to____ all the chil - dren.

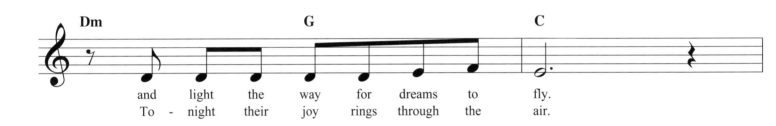

and light the way for dreams to fly.
To - night their joy rings through the air.

To - night our love comes wrapped in____ rib - bons.
And so, we send our ten - der bless - ings

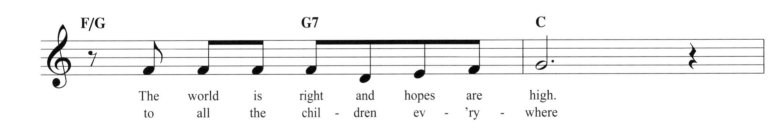

The world is right and hopes are high.
to all the chil - dren ev - 'ry - where

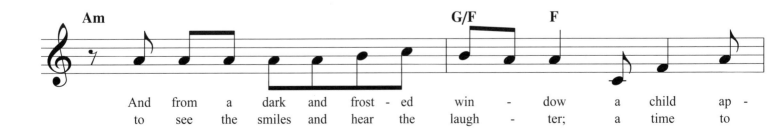

And from a dark and frost - ed win - dow a child ap -
to see the smiles and hear the laugh - ter; a time to

pears ____ to search the sky ____ be - cause it's
give, ____ a time to share ____ be - cause it's

Christ - mas, ____ be - cause it's Christ - mas.

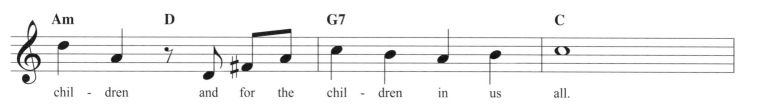

Christ - mas for now____ and for - ev - er for all____ of the

chil - dren and for the chil - dren in us all.

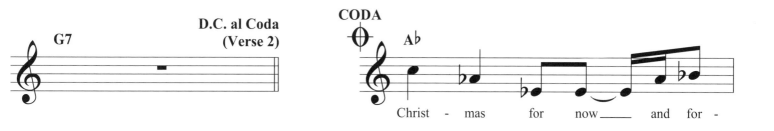

G7   **D.C. al Coda** (Verse 2)   **CODA**   Ab

Christ - mas for now____ and for -

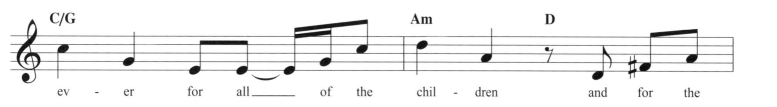

ev - er for all____ of the chil - dren and for the

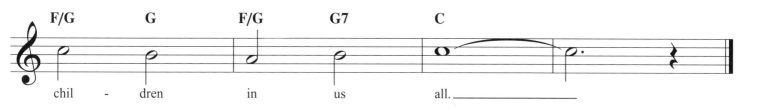

chil - dren in us all.____

BELIEVE
from Warner Bros. Pictures' THE POLAR EXPRESS

Words and Music by GLEN BALLARD
and ALAN SILVESTRI

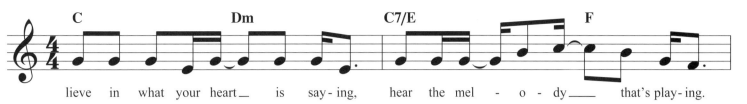

lieve in what your heart is say-ing, hear the mel - o - dy that's play-ing.

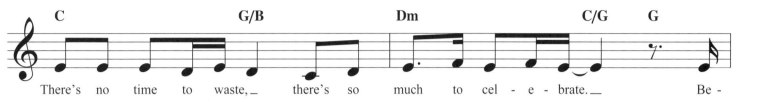

There's no time to waste, there's so much to cel - e - brate. Be -

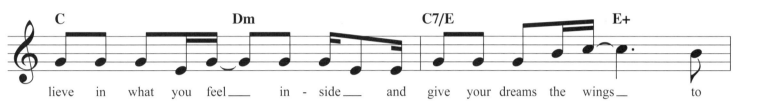

lieve in what you feel in - side and give your dreams the wings to

fly. You have ev - 'ry - thing you need if you just

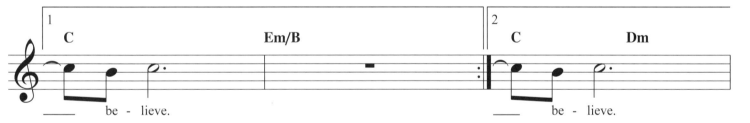

be - lieve.   be - lieve.

If you just be - lieve, if you just

be - lieve. If you just be - lieve.

Just be - lieve, just be - lieve.

Blue Christmas

Words and Music by BILLY HAYES
and JAY JOHNSON

With expression

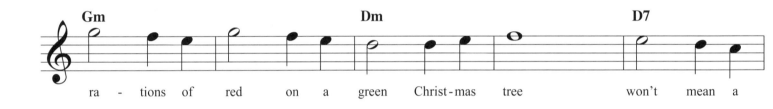

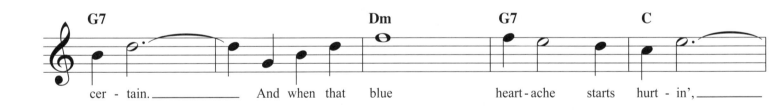

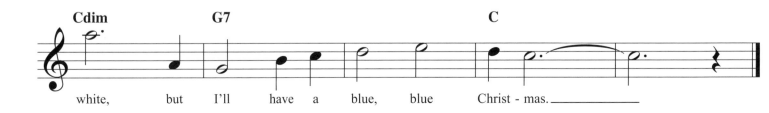

BREATH OF HEAVEN
(Mary's Song)

Words and Music by AMY GRANT
and CHRIS EATON

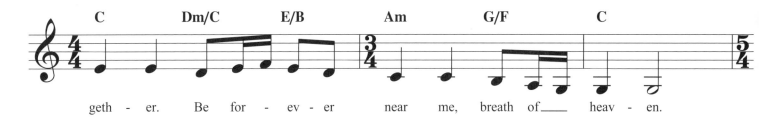

geth - er. Be for - ev - er near me, breath of____ heav - en.

Breath of heav - en, light - en my dark - ness. Pour o - ver me Your

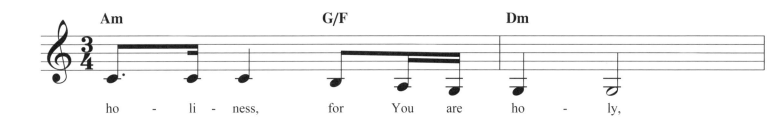

ho - li - ness, for You are ho - ly,

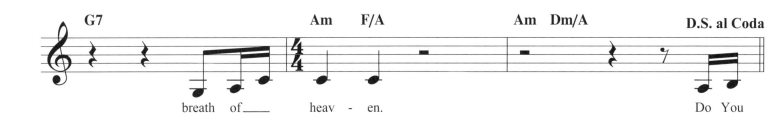

breath of____ heav - en. Do You

plan._____ Help____ me be strong,____ help____ me be,____

____ help____ me. Breath of heav - en, hold me to-

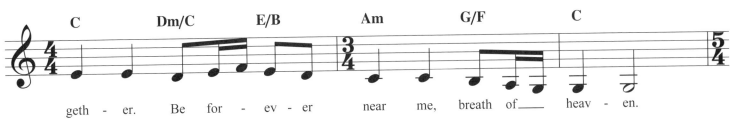

geth - er. Be for - ev - er near me, breath of___ heav - en.

Breath of heav - en, light - en my dark - ness. Pour o - ver me Your

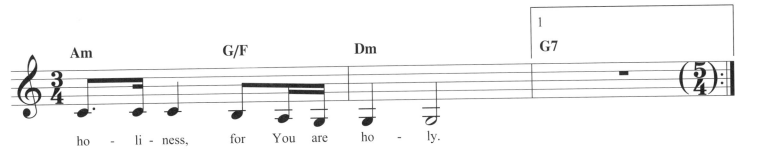

ho - li - ness, for You are ho - ly.

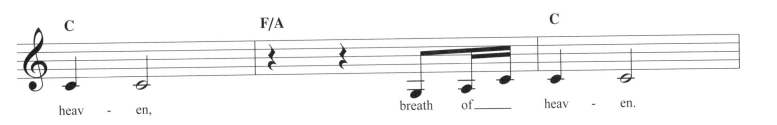

Breath of___ heav - en, breath of___

heav - en, breath of___ heav - en.

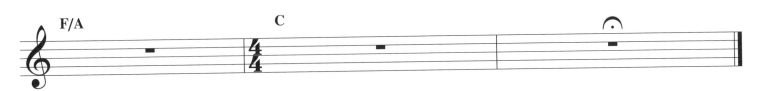

BRAZILIAN SLEIGH BELLS

By PERCY FAITH

Bright Samba

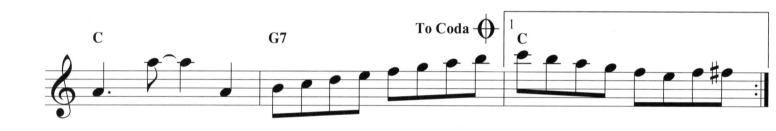

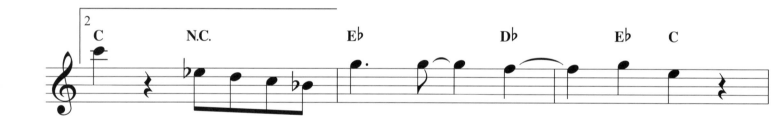

A CHILD IS BORN

Music by THAD JONES
Lyrics by ALEC WILDER

THE CHIPMUNK SONG

Words and Music by
ROSS BAGDASARIAN

Moderately

Christ - mas, Christ - mas time is near, time for

toys and time for cheer. We've been good but

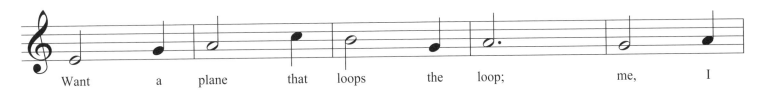

we can't last. Hur - ry, Christ - mas, hur - ry fast!

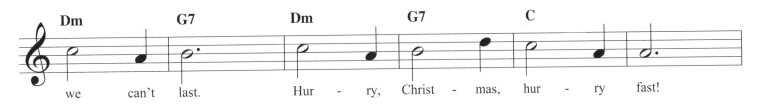

Want a plane that loops the loop; me, I

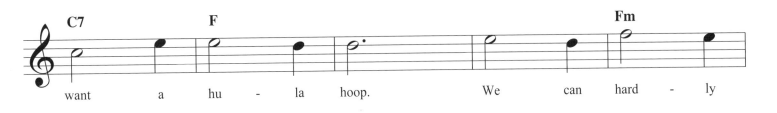

want a hu - la hoop. We can hard - ly

stand the wait. Please, Christ - mas, don't be late. _____

CHRISTMAS AULD LANG SYNE

Words and Music by MANN CURTIS
and FRANK MILITARY

Hymn style

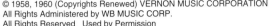

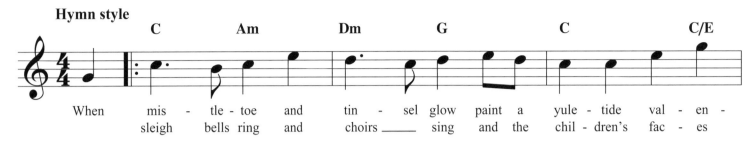

When mis - tle - toe and tin - sel glow paint a yule - tide val - en -
sleigh bells ring and choirs ____ sing and the chil - dren's fac - es

tine, back home I go to those I know ____ for a
shine, with each new toy we share their joy ____ with a

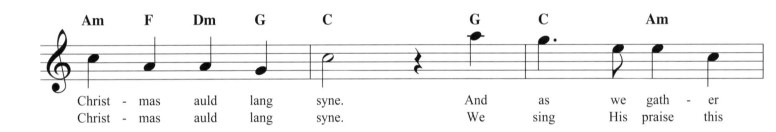

Christ - mas auld lang syne. And as we gath - er
Christ - mas auld lang syne. We sing His praise this

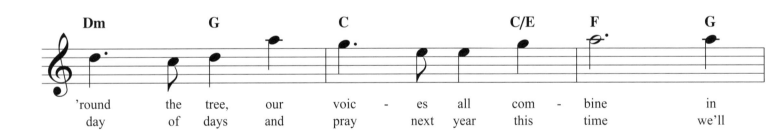

'round the tree, our voic - es all com - bine in
day of days and pray next year this time we'll

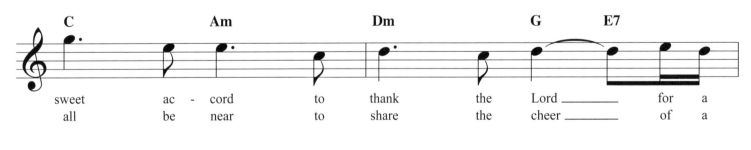

sweet ac - cord to thank the Lord ____ for a
all be near to share the cheer ____ of a

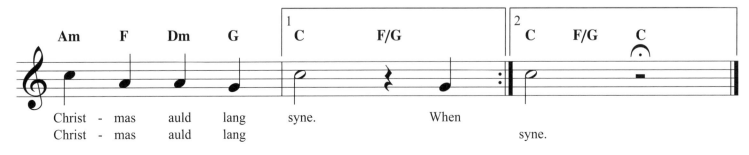

1.
Christ - mas auld lang syne. When

2.
Christ - mas auld lang syne.

CHRISTMAS IN KILLARNEY

Words and Music by JOHN REDMOND
and FRANK WELDON

Moderately, with a lilt

The hol-ly green, the i-vy green, the pret-ti-est pic-ture you've ev-er seen is

Christ-mas in Kil-lar-ney, with all of the folks at home. It's nice you know, to kiss your beau while

cud-dling un-der the mis-tle-toe, and San-ta Claus, you know of course, is

one of the boys from home. The door is al-ways o-pen, the neigh-bors pay a call, and

Fa-ther John, be-fore he's gone, will bless the house and all. How

grand it feels, to click your heels and join in the fun of the jigs and reels. I'm

hand-ing you no blar-ney, the likes you've nev-er known is

Christ-mas in Kil-lar-ney, with all of the folks at home.

CHRISTMAS
(Baby Please Come Home)

Words and Music by PHIL SPECTOR,
ELLIE GREENWICH and JEFF BARRY

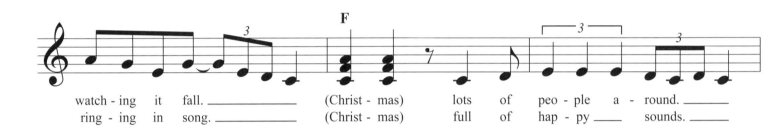

CHRISTMAS IS

Lyrics by SPENCE MAXWELL
Music by PERCY FAITH

Slowly

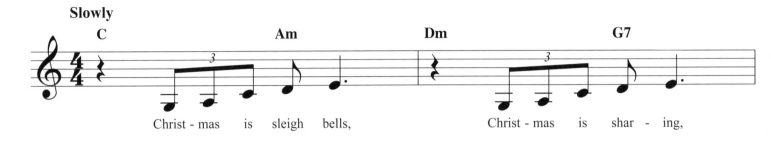

Christ - mas is sleigh bells,   Christ - mas is shar - ing,

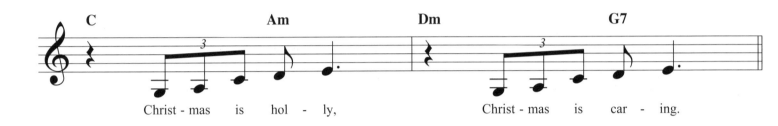

Christ - mas is hol - ly,   Christ - mas is car - ing.

Christ - mas is chil - dren who just can't___ go to sleep,
Christ - mas is car - ols to warm you___ in the snow,

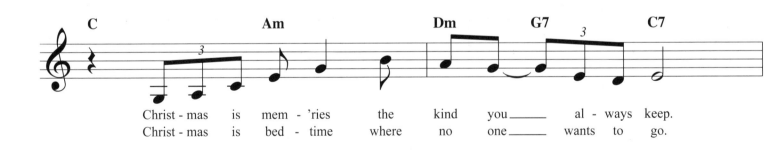

Christ - mas is mem - 'ries the kind you___ al - ways keep.
Christ - mas is bed - time where no one___ wants to go.

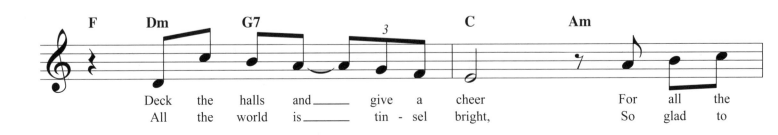

Deck the halls and___ give a cheer,   For all the
All the world is___ tin - sel bright,   So glad to

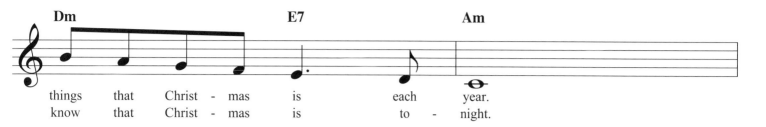

things that Christ - mas is each year.
know that Christ - mas is to - night.

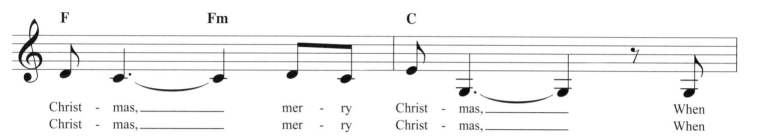

Christ - mas,_____ mer - ry Christ - mas,_____ When
Christ - mas,_____ mer - ry Christ - mas,_____ When

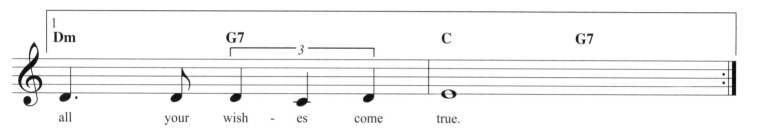

all your wish - es come true.

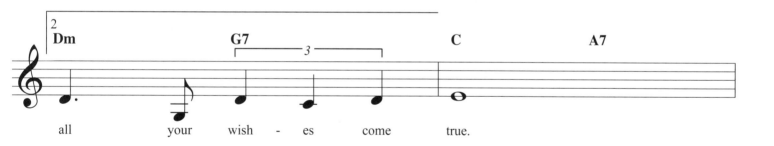

all your wish - es come true.

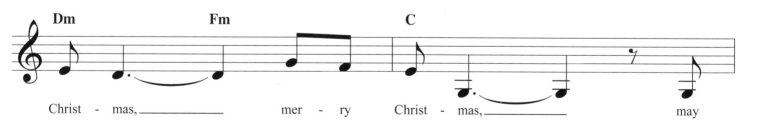

Christ - mas,_____ mer - ry Christ - mas,_____ may

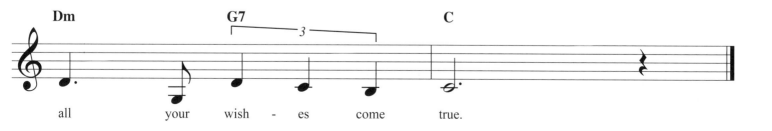

all your wish - es come true.

CHRISTMAS IS A-COMIN'
(May God Bless You)

Words and Music by
FRANK LUTHER

Moderately slow

When I'm feel - in' blue, an' when I'm feel - in' low,

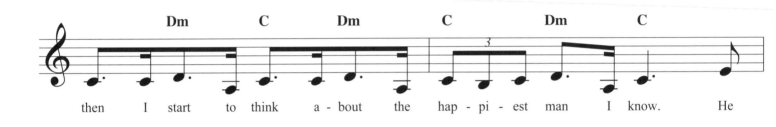

then I start to think a - bout the hap - pi - est man I know. He

does - n't mind the snow an' he does - n't mind the rain, but

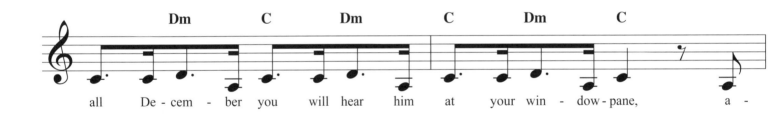

all De - cem - ber you will hear him at your win - dow - pane, a -

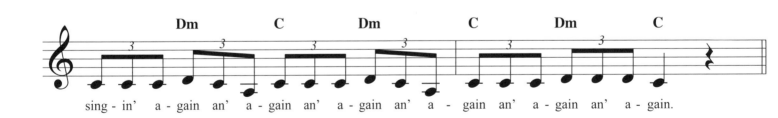

sing - in' a - gain an' a - gain an' a - gain an' a - gain an' a - gain an' a - gain.

Christ - mas is a - com - in' and the geese are get - tin' fat,
Christ - mas is a - com - in' and the lights are on the tree,
Christ - mas is a - com - in' and the egg is in the nog,

CHRISTMAS LIGHTS

Words and Music by GUY BERRYMAN,
WILL CHAMPION, CHRIS MARTIN
and JONNY BUCKLAND

THE CHRISTMAS SHOES

Words and Music by LEONARD AHLSTROM
and EDDIE CARSWELL

37

38

-en's love ____ as he thanked me and __ ran out. ____ I knew that

God had sent ____ that lit - tle boy to re - mind me _____

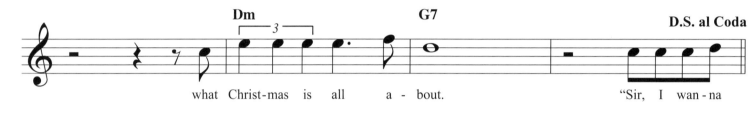

what Christ-mas is all a - bout. "Sir, I wan - na

night. I want her to ____ look beau-

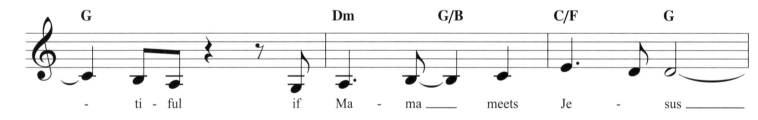

- ti - ful if Ma - ma ____ meets Je - sus _____

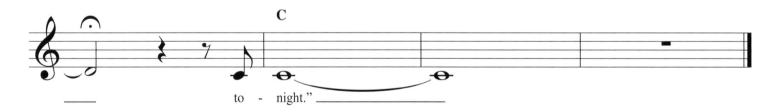

____ to - night." _____

Additional Verse

2. They counted pennies for what seemed like years,
   Then the cashier said, "Son, there's not enough here."
   He searched his pockets frantic'lly,
   Then he turned and he looked at me.
   He said, "Mama made Christmas good at our house,
   Though most years she just did without.
   Tell me, sir, what am I gonna do?
   Somehow I've gotta buy her these Christmas shoes."
   So, I laid the money down.
   I just had to help him out.
   And I'll never forget the look on his face when he said,
   "Mama's gonna look so great."
   Chorus

CHRISTMAS TIME IS HERE
from A CHARLIE BROWN CHRISTMAS

Words by Lee Mendelson
Music by VINCE GUARALDI

THE CHRISTMAS SONG
(Chestnuts Roasting on an Open Fire)

Music and Lyric by MEL TORMÉ
and ROBERT WELLS

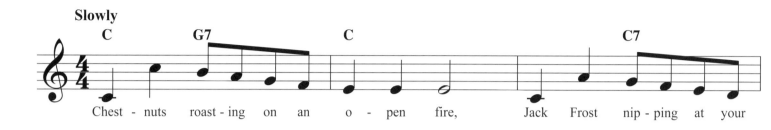

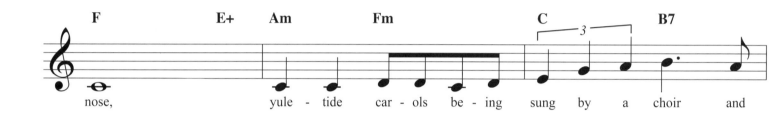

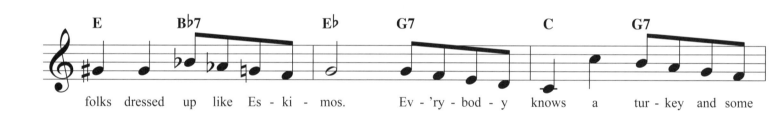

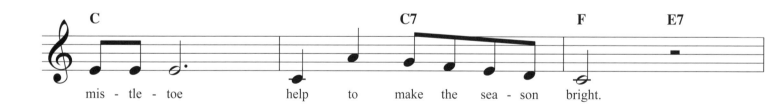

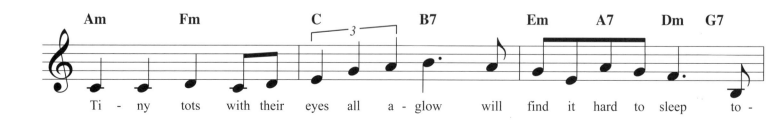

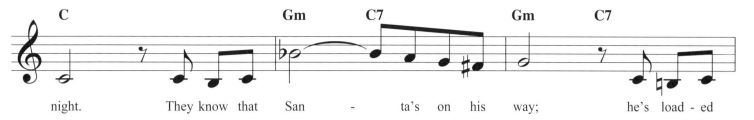

night. They know that San - ta's on his way; he's load - ed

lots of toys and good - ies on his sleigh, and ev - 'ry moth - er's child ___ is gon - na

spy _____ to see if rein - deer ___ real - ly know how to

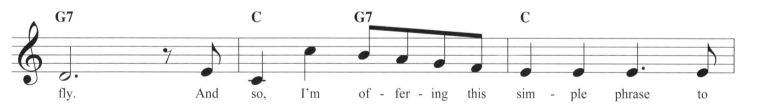

fly. And so, I'm of - fer - ing this sim - ple phrase to

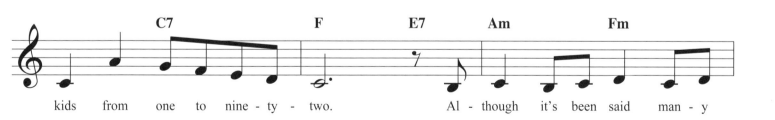

kids from one to nine - ty - two. Al - though it's been said man - y

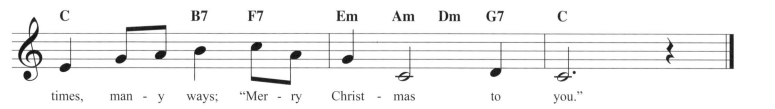

times, man - y ways; "Mer - ry Christ - mas to you."

THE CHRISTMAS WALTZ

Words by SAMMY CAHN
Music by JULE STYNE

DO THEY KNOW IT'S CHRISTMAS?
(Feed the World)

Words and Music by BOB GELDOF
and MIDGE URE

It's Christ - mas - time, there's no need to be a - fraid. __

At Christ - mas - time, we let in light __ and we ban - ish shade. __

And in our world __ of plen - ty __ we can

spread a smile __ of joy. __ Throw your arms __ a - round __ the world __

__ at Christ - mas - time. __ But say a prayer,

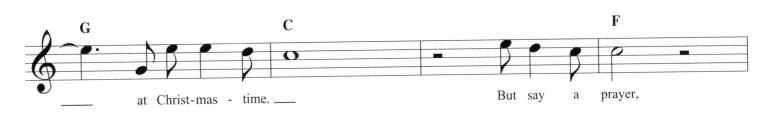

to pray for the oth - er ones __ at Christ - mas - time. __ It's

hard, but __ when you're hav - ing fun __ there's __ a __ world out - side your win -

44

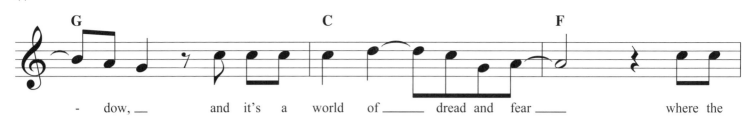

-dow, __ and it's a world of ____ dread and fear ____ where the

on - ly wa - ter flow-ing is ____ the bit - ter sting of

tears. And the Christ-mas bells __ that ring ____ there __ are the

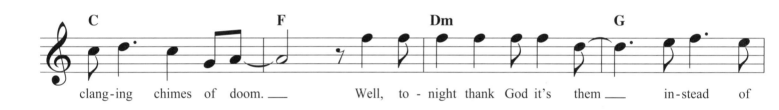

clang-ing chimes of doom. __ Well, to - night thank God it's them __ in-stead of

you. And there won't be snow __ in Af - ri - ca ____ this Christ -

- mas - time, __ the great-est gift __ they'll get this year ____ is life. __

____ Oh. _____ Where noth-ing ev - er grows, __ no

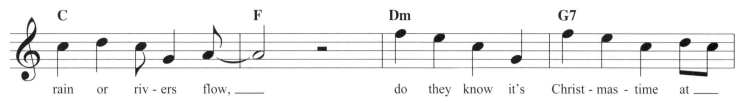

rain or riv - ers flow, ____ do they know it's Christ - mas - time at ___

all? Here's to you, raise a glass for ev - 'ry - one;

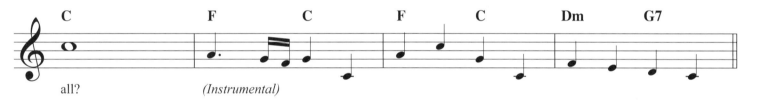

here's to them un - der - neath that burn - ing sun. Do they know it's Christ - mas - time at ___

all? *(Instrumental)*

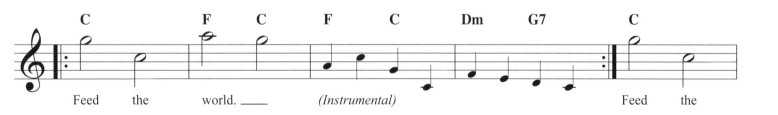

Feed the world. ___ *(Instrumental)* Feed the

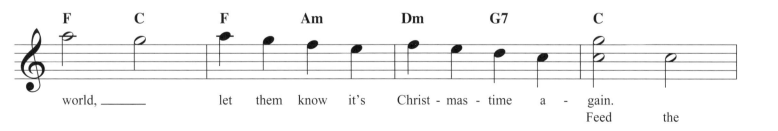

world, _____ let them know it's Christ - mas - time a - gain.
Feed the

world, ____ Let them know it's Christ - mas - time a - gain. _____

CHRISTMAS WRAPPING

Words and Music by
CHRIS BUTLER

Bah, hum - bug! No, that's too strong 'cause it is my fa - v'rite hol - i - day. __ But all this year's been a bus - y blur. Don't think I have the en - er - gy __ to add to my __ al - read - y mad rush just 'cause this is the sea - son. The per - fect gift for me would be __ com - ple - tions and con - nec - tions left from last year's ski - shop en - coun - ter, most in - t'rest - ing. __ Had his num - ber, but nev - er the time. __ Most of eight - y - one passed a - long those lines. So, deck those halls, trim those trees, __ raise up cups of Christ - mas cheer. __ I just need to catch __ my breath. Christ - mas by __ my - self __ this

year. *(Instrumental)*

Cal - en - dar pic - tures, fro - zen land - scape

chilled this room for twen - ty - four days. Ev - er - greens, spar - kl - ing snow;

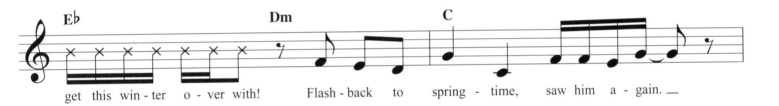

get this win - ter o - ver with! Flash - back to spring - time, saw him a - gain. __

Would -'ve been good to go __ for lunch. Could - n't a - gree we're both free. We

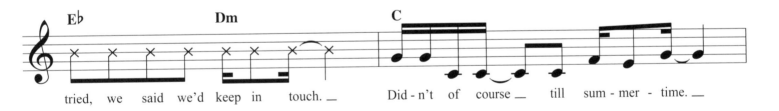

tried, we said we'd keep in touch. __ Did - n't of course __ till sum - mer - time. __

Out to the beach to his boat, could I join him? No! This time it was me, __

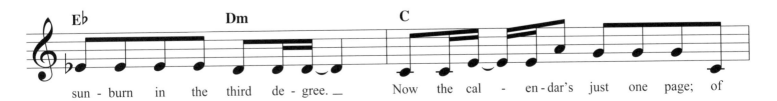

sun - burn in the third de - gree. __ Now the cal - en - dar's just one page; of

course I am ex - cit - ed.

F/C To - night's the night __ I set my mind not to

N.C. do too much __ a - bout _____ it. *(Instrumental)*

C

Gm **Am/C** **C**

Mer - ry Christ - mas, Mer - ry Christ - mas, { (1.,2.) but I / (3.,4.) }

1, 3

think I'll miss __ this one __ this year. __ } Mer - ry Christ - mas, Mer - ry Christ - mas, { but I
could - n't miss __ this one __ this year. __ }

2, 4 **Last time To Coda**

think I'll miss __ this one __ this year. __ } Mer - ry Christ - mas, Mer - ry Christ - mas, { but I
could - n't miss __ this one __ this year. __ }

think I'll miss __ this one __ this year. A & P ___ has pride in me with the

F/C world's small - est tur - key. Al - read - y in the ov - en, nice __ and hot. __ Oh,

damn! Guess what I ____ for - got! So on with the boots, back out in the snow to the

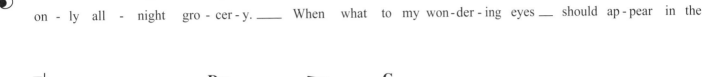

on - ly all - night gro - cer - y. ____ When what to my won - der - ing eyes ___ should ap - pear in the

line is that guy I've been chas - in' all year! "I'm spend - ing this one a - lone," _ he said. "Need a

break; this year's been cra - zy." I said, "Me too, but why are you...? You mean

you for - got ___ cran - ber - ries too?" _ Then sud - den - ly ____ we laughed ___ and laughed, _ caught

on to what was hap - pen - ing. __ That Christ - mas mag - ic's brought this tale to a ver - y hap - py end -

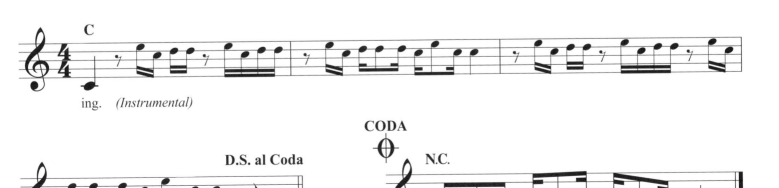

ing. (Instrumental)

D.S. al Coda

CODA

N.C.

could - n't miss __ this one __ this year. __

CHRISTMASES WHEN YOU WERE MINE

Words and Music by NATHAN CHAPMAN,
LIZ ROSE and TAYLOR SWIFT

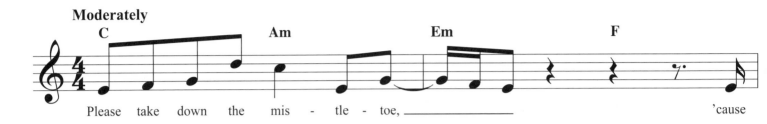

Please take down the mis - tle - toe, _____ 'cause

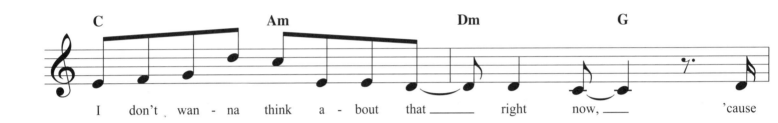

I don't wan - na think a - bout that _____ right now, _____ 'cause

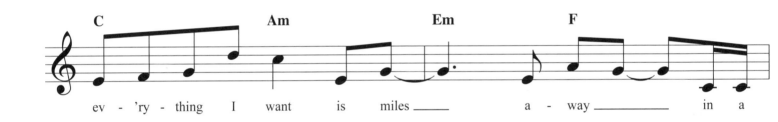

ev - 'ry - thing I want is miles _____ a - way _____ in a

snow - cov - ered lit - tle town. My

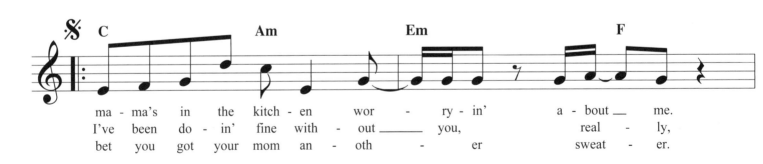

ma - ma's in the kitch - en wor - ry - in' a - bout _ me.
I've been do - in' fine with - out _____ you, real - ly,
bet you got your mom an - oth - er sweat - er.

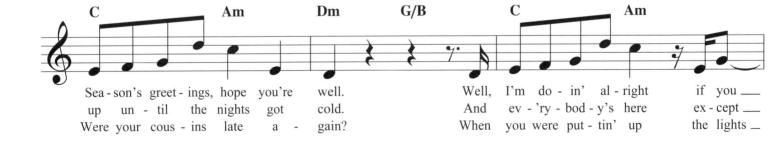

Sea - son's greet - ings, hope you're well. Well, I'm do - in' al - right if you _____
up un - til the nights got cold. And ev - 'ry - bod - y's here ex - cept
Were your cous - ins late a - gain? When you were put - tin' up the lights

51

CHRISTMASTIME

Words and Music by MICHAEL W. SMITH
and JOANNA CARLSON

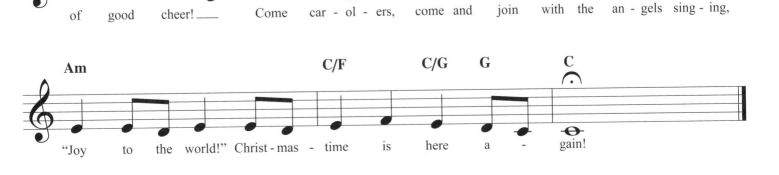

COLD DECEMBER NIGHTS

Words and Music by SHAWN STOCKMAN
and MICHAEL McCARY

DO YOU HEAR WHAT I HEAR

Words and Music by NOEL REGNEY
and GLORIA SHAYNE

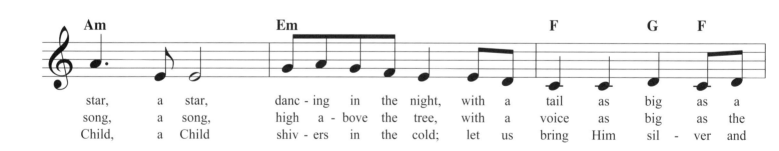

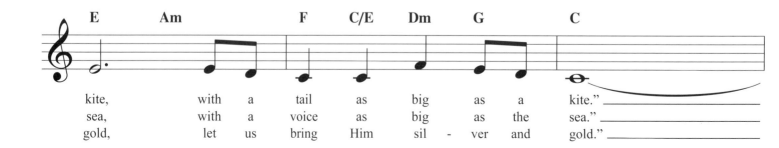

1, 2 — Said the
Said the

3 — Said the king to the peo - ple ev - 'ry -

where, "Lis - ten to what I say! _____

Pray for peace, peo - ple ev - 'ry - where, lis - ten to what I say! __

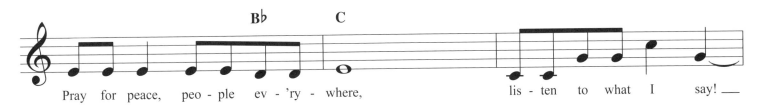

____ The Child, the Child, sleep - ing in the night. He will

bring us good - ness and light, He will bring us

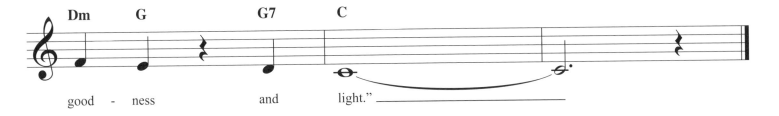

good - ness and light." _____

DO YOU WANT TO BUILD A SNOWMAN?
from FROZEN

Music and Lyrics by KRISTEN ANDERSON-LOPEZ
and ROBERT LOPEZ

Moderate-rhythmic but expressive

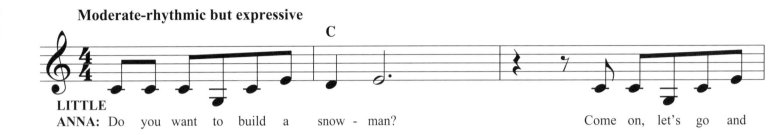

LITTLE
ANNA: Do you want to build a snow-man? Come on, let's go and

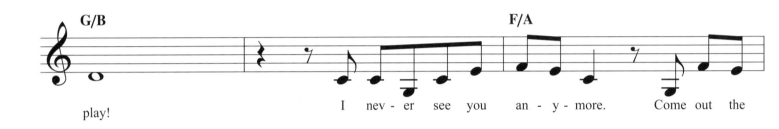

play! I nev-er see you an-y-more. Come out the

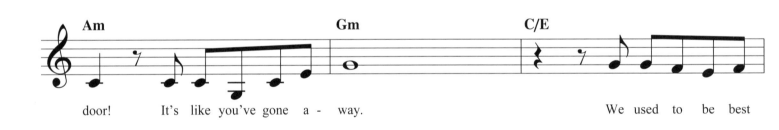

door! It's like you've gone a-way. We used to be best

bud-dies, and now we're not. ___ I wish you would tell me

why. Do you want to build a snow-man?

It does - n't have to be a snow - man.   **LITTLE ELSA:** *(Spoken:)* Go away, Anna.

A little faster

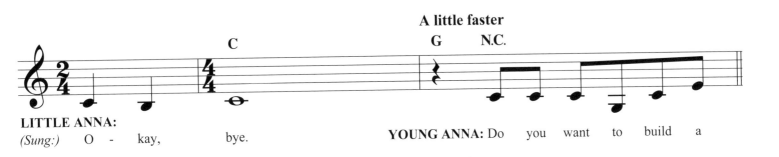

LITTLE ANNA:
(Sung:) O - kay,   bye.   **YOUNG ANNA:** Do   you   want   to   build   a

snow - man?   Or   ride   our   bikes   a - round   the   halls?

I   think   some   com - pan - y   is   o - ver - due;   I've   start - ed

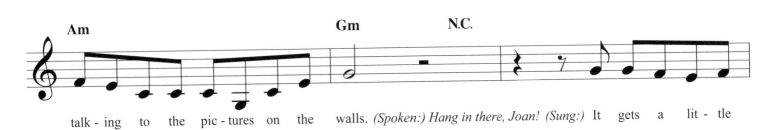

talk - ing   to   the   pic - tures   on   the   walls. *(Spoken:)* Hang in there, Joan! *(Sung:)* It   gets   a   lit - tle

lone - ly,   all these   emp - ty ____ rooms, ____   just   watch - ing   the   hours   tick

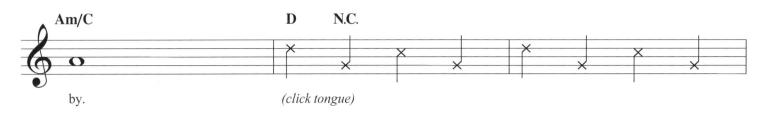

by.

(click tongue)

A little slower, tenderly

(knocking) **ANNA:** *(Spoken:) Elsa? (Sung:)* Please, I know you're in there.

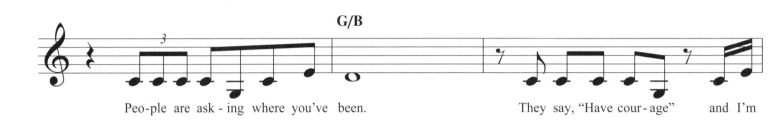

Peo-ple are ask-ing where you've been. They say, "Have cour-age" and I'm

try-ing to; I'm right out here for you, just let me in.

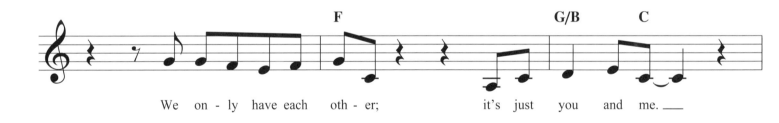

We on-ly have each oth-er; it's just you and me. ___

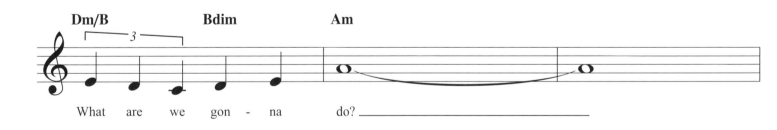

What are we gon-na do? _____

Slower

Do you want to build a snow-man? _____

FAIRYTALE OF NEW YORK

Words and Music by JEREMY FINER
and SHANE MacGOWAN

Male: 1. It was Christ - mas Eve, ___ babe, in the drunk tank, when an old man
2. *(See additional lyrics)*

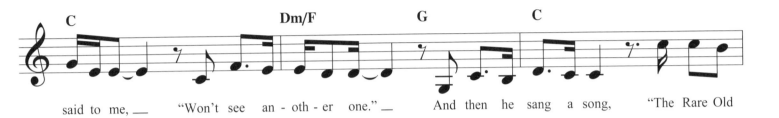

said to me, ___ "Won't see an - oth - er one." ___ And then he sang a song, "The Rare Old

Moun - tain Dew." I turned my face a - way ___ and dreamed a - bout you. 2. Got on a

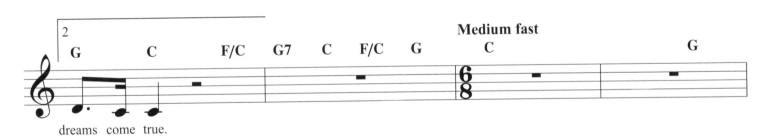

dreams come true.

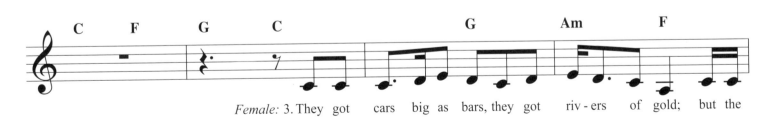

Female: 3. They got cars big as bars, they got riv - ers of gold; but the

wind goes right through you, it's no place for the old. ___ When you

first took my hand on a cold ___ Christ - mas Eve, you prom - ised me Broad - way was

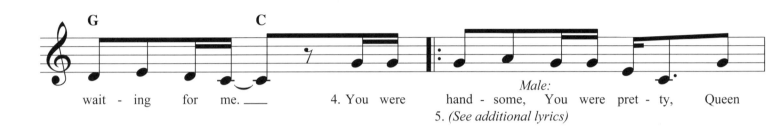

wait - ing for me. ___ 4. You were hand - some, You were pret - ty, Queen

5. *(See additional lyrics)*

Male:

Both:

of New York Cit - y. When the band fin - ished play - ing, they howled out for more. ___ Si -

na - tra was swing - ing; all the drunks, they were sing - ing. We kissed on the cor - ner, then

danced through the night. ___ The boys of the N - Y - P - D choir ___ were

sing - ing ___ "Gal - way Bay." And the bells ___ were ring - ing out ___

Additional Lyrics

2. Got on a lucky one, came in eighteen to one;
   I've got a feeling this year's for me and you.
   So happy Christmas; I love you, baby.
   I can see a better time when all our dreams come true.

5. *(Female)* You're a bum, you're a punk!
   (Male) You're an old slut on junk
   Lying there almost dead on a drip in that bed!
   (Female) You scumbag! You maggot!
   You cheap lousy faggot!
   Happy Christmas your arse!
   I pray God it's our last.

FELIZ NAVIDAD

Music and Lyrics by
JOSÉ FELICIANO

Fe - liz Na - vi - dad. ____ Fe - liz Na - vi - dad. ____ Fe - liz Na - vi-

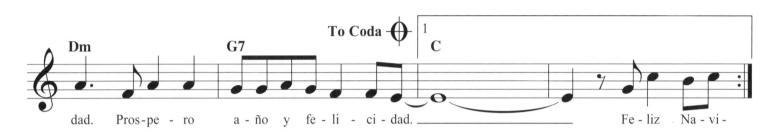

dad. Pros - pe - ro   a - ño y fe - li - ci - dad. ____ Fe - liz   Na - vi-

__ I want to wish you a Mer - ry Christ-mas,   with lots of pres - ents to

make you hap - py.   I want to wish you a Mer - ry Christ-mas from the bot-tom of my

heart. ____   I want to wish you a Mer - ry Christ-mas,   with mis - tle - toe and _

lots of cheer, _   with lots of laugh-ter through-out the years from the bot-tom of my

heart. ____   Fe - liz Na - vi -

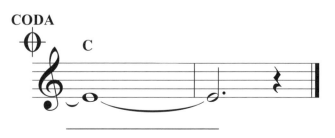

THE GREATEST GIFT OF ALL

Words and Music by
JOHN JARVIS

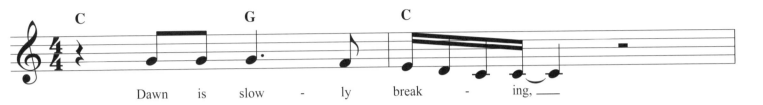

Dawn is slow - ly break - ing, ___

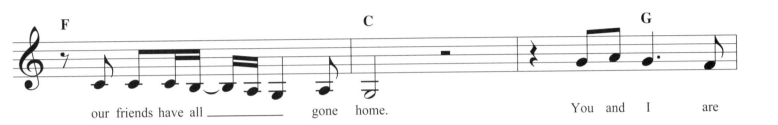

our friends have all _____ gone home.   You and I are

wait - ing ___   for San - ta Claus to

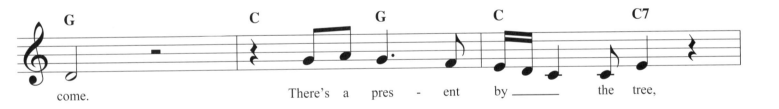

come.   There's a pres - ent by _____ the tree,

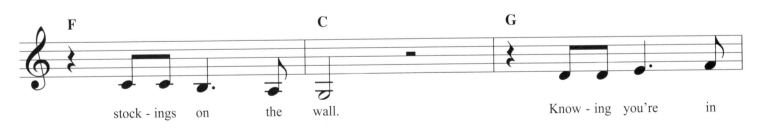

stock - ings on the wall.   Know - ing you're in

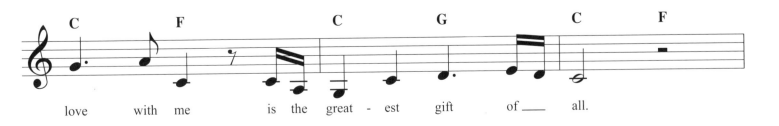

love with me is the great - est gift of ___ all.

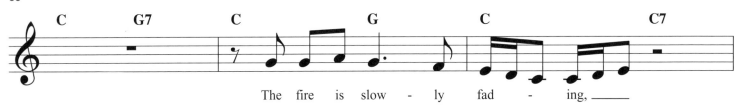

The fire is slow - ly fad - ing, _____

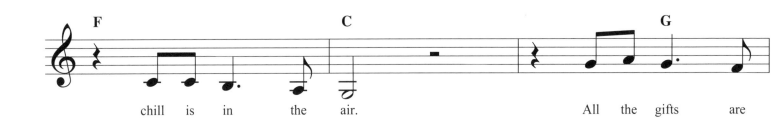

chill is in the air. All the gifts are

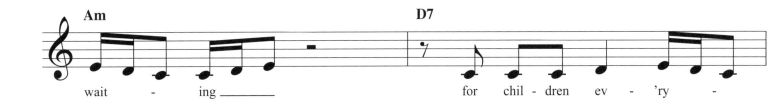

wait - ing _____ for chil - dren ev - 'ry -

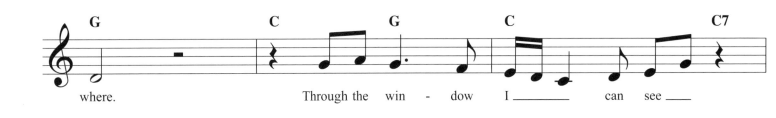

where. Through the win - dow I _____ can see _____

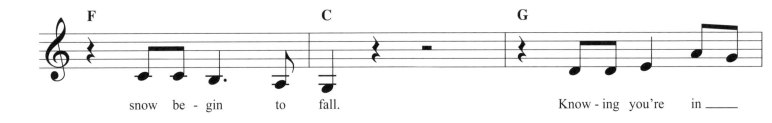

snow be - gin to fall. Know - ing you're in _____

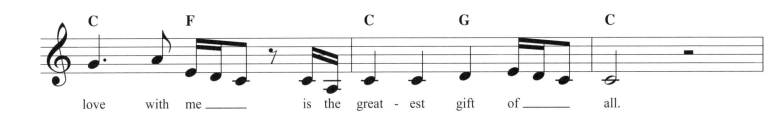

love with me _____ is the great - est gift of _____ all.

Just be - fore I go to sleep _____

I hear a church bell ring. Mer - ry Christ - mas

ev - 'ry - one _____ is the song it _____ sings.

So I say a si - lent prayer _____ for crea - tures great and

small. Peace on Earth good _____ will to men is the

great - est gift of _____ all. Peace on Earth good _____

will to men is the great - est gift of _____

all. _____

FROSTY THE SNOW MAN

Words and Music by STEVE NELSON
and JACK ROLLINS

Moderately

Frost - y the Snow Man was a jol - ly hap - py soul, ___
Frost - y the Snow Man knew the sun was hot that day, ___

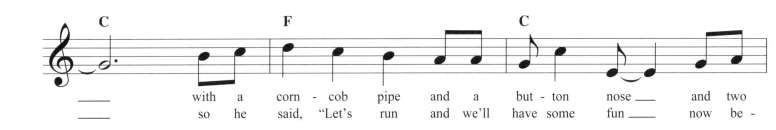

___ with a corn - cob pipe and a but - ton nose ___ and two
___ so he said, "Let's run and we'll have some fun ___ now be -

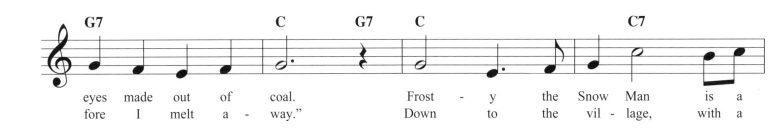

eyes made out of coal. Frost - y the Snow Man is a
fore I melt a - way." Down to the vil - lage, with a

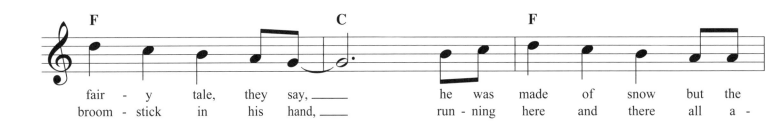

fair - y tale, they say, ___ he was made of snow but the
broom - stick in his hand, ___ run - ning here and there all a -

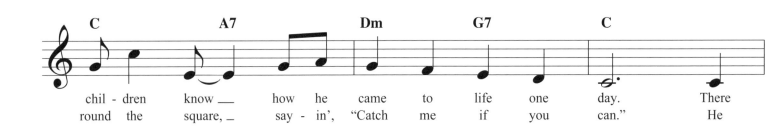

chil - dren know ___ how he came to life one day. There
round the square, ___ say - in', "Catch me if you can." He

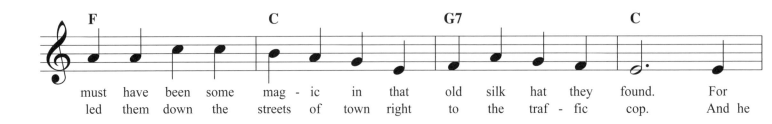

must have been some mag - ic in that old silk hat they found. For
led them down the streets of town right to the traf - fic cop. And he

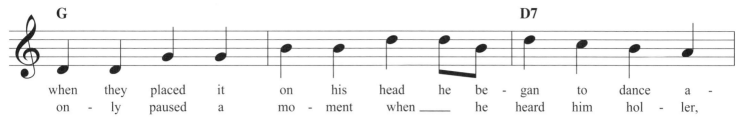

G ... **D7**

when they placed it on his head he be - gan to dance a -
on - ly paused a mo - ment when ____ he heard him hol - ler,

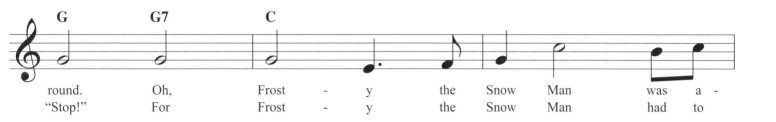

G **G7** **C**

round. Oh, Frost - y the Snow Man was a -
"Stop!" For Frost - y the Snow Man had to

F **C** **F**

live as he could be, _____ and the chil - dren say he could
hur - ry on his way, _____ but he waved good - bye say - in'

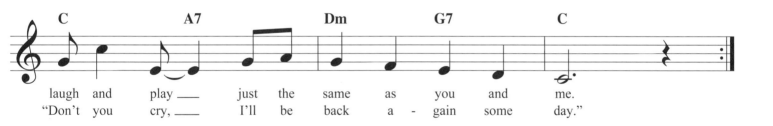

C **A7** **Dm** **G7** **C**

laugh and play ___ just the same as you and me.
"Don't you cry, ___ I'll be back a - gain some day."

C **G7**

Thump-et - y thump thump, thump-et - y thump thump. Look at Frost - y go.

C **C**

Thump-et - y thump thump, thump-et - y thump thump. O - ver the hills of snow.

GRANDMA GOT RUN OVER BY A REINDEER

Words and Music by
RANDY BROOKS

Moderately bright

Chorus

Grand-ma got run o - ver by a rein-deer walk-ing home from our house Christ-mas

Eve. You can say there's no such thing as San - ta, but

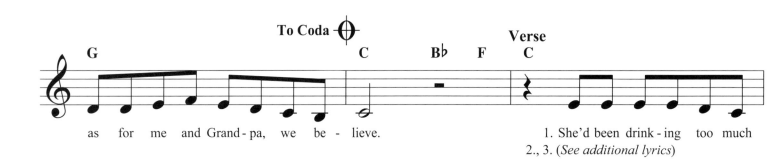

To Coda ⊕   **Verse**

as for me and Grand-pa, we be - lieve. 1. She'd been drink-ing too much
2., 3. *(See additional lyrics)*

egg - nog and we begged her not to go,

but she for-got her med-i - ca-tion, and she stag-gered out the door in-to the

snow. When we found her Christ-mas morn - ing

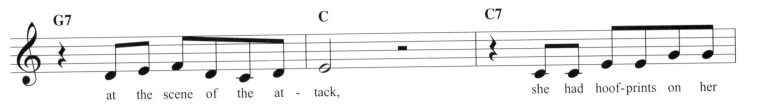

at the scene of the at - tack, she had hoof-prints on her

1st and 2nd time D.C.
3rd time D.C. al Coda

fore - head, and in - crim - i - nat - ing Claus marks on her back.

CODA

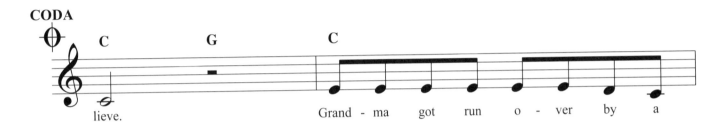

lieve. Grand - ma got run o - ver by a

rein - deer walk - ing home from our house Christ - mas Eve.

You can say there's no such thing as San - ta, but as for me and Grand - pa, we be -

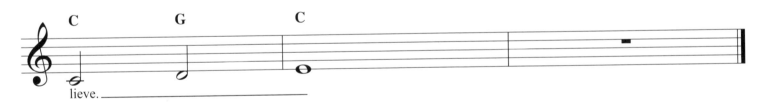

lieve. _____

Additional Lyrics

2. Now we're all so proud of Grandpa,
   He's been taking this so well.
   See him in there watching football,
   Drinking beer and playing cards with Cousin Mel.
   It's not Christmas without Grandma.
   All the family's dressed in black,
   And we just can't help but wonder;
   Should we open up her gifts or send them back?
   Chorus

3. Now the goose is on the table,
   And the pudding made of fig,
   And the blue and silver candles,
   That would just have matched the hair in Grandma's wig.
   I've warned all my friends and neighbors,
   Better watch out for yourselves.
   They should never give a license
   To a man who drives a sleigh and plays with elves.
   Chorus

GROWN-UP CHRISTMAS LIST

Words and Music by DAVID FOSTER
and LINDA THOMPSON-JENNER

Moderately slow

Do you re-mem-ber me? I sat up-on ___ your knee. ___ I
wrote to you with child-hood fan-ta-sies.
Well, I'm all grown ___ up now, and
chil-dren we ___ be-lieved the

still need help some-how. I'm not a child, ___ but my heart still can dream. So
grand-est sight to see was some-thing love - ly wrapped be-neath our tree. Well,

here's my life-long wish, my grown-up Christ-mas list, not for my-self, ___ but for a world ___ in
heav-en sure-ly knows that pack-ag-es and bows can nev-er heal ___ a hurt-ing hu-man

need.)
soul.)
No more lives ___ torn a-part, ___ and wars would nev - er start, ___

___ and time would heal ___ all hearts. And ev - 'ry-one would have ___ a friend, ___

and right would al - ways win, and love would nev - er end. ___

HAPPY HOLIDAY
from the Motion Picture Irving Berlin's HOLIDAY INN

Words and Music by
IRVING BERLIN

HERE COMES SANTA CLAUS
(Right Down Santa Claus Lane)

Words and Music by GENE AUTRY
and OAKLEY HALDEMAN

Here comes San - ta Claus! Here comes San - ta Claus! Right down San - ta Claus Lane!

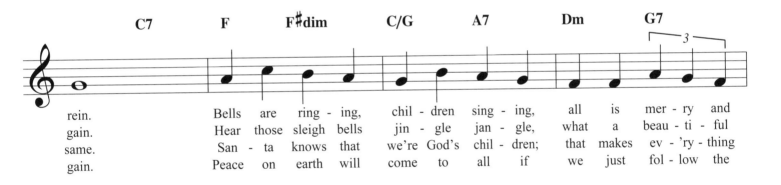

Vix - en and Blitz - en and all his rein - deer are pull - ing on the
He's got a bag that is all filled with toys for the boys and girls a -
He does - n't care if you're rich or poor, for he loves you just the
He'll come a - round when the chimes ring out; then it's Christ - mas morn a -

rein.   Bells are ring - ing, chil - dren sing - ing, all is mer - ry and
gain.   Hear those sleigh bells jin - gle jan - gle, what a beau - ti - ful
same.   San - ta knows that we're God's chil - dren; that makes ev - 'ry - thing
gain.   Peace on earth will come to all if we just fol - low the

bright.   Hang your stock - ings and say your pray'rs, }
sight.   Jump in bed, cov - er up your head, } 'cause
right.   Fill your hearts with a Christ - mas cheer,
light.   Let's give thanks to the Lord a - bove,

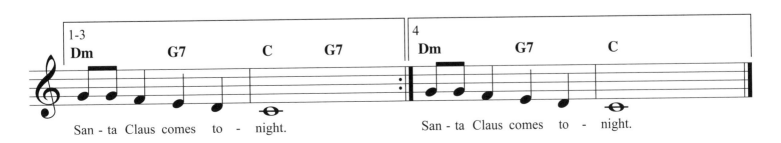

1-3
San - ta Claus comes to - night.

4
San - ta Claus comes to - night.

HAPPY XMAS
(War Is Over)

Written by JOHN LENNON
and YOKO ONO

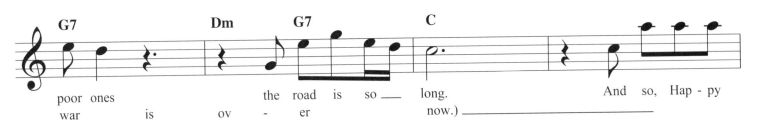

poor ones ... the road is so __ long. And so, Hap - py
war is ov - er now.) _____

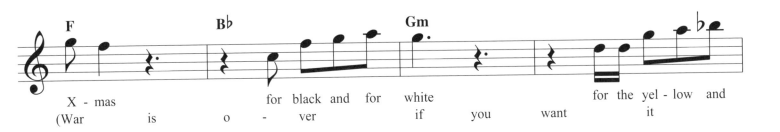

X - mas ... for black and for white ... for the yel - low and
(War is o - ver if you want it

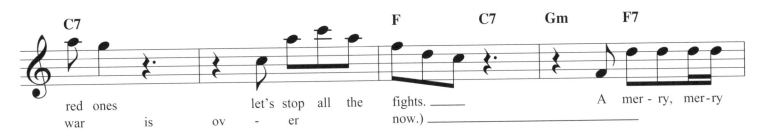

red ones ... let's stop all the fights. ___ A mer - ry, mer-ry
war is ov - er now.) _____

X - mas ___ and a hap - py New Year, let's hope it's a

good one ___ with - out an - y fear. And so this is

CODA

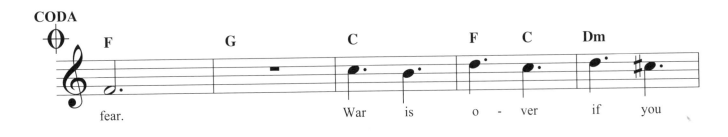

fear. War is o - ver if you

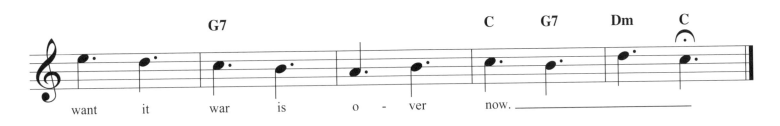

want it war is o - ver now. _____

HARD CANDY CHRISTMAS
from THE BEST LITTLE WHOREHOUSE IN TEXAS

Words and Music by
CAROL HALL

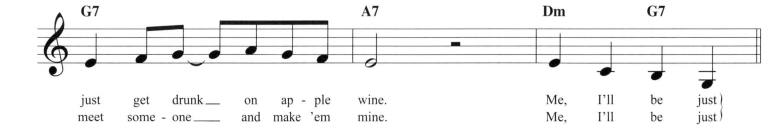

HAVE YOURSELF A MERRY LITTLE CHRISTMAS

from MEET ME IN ST. LOUIS

Words and Music by HUGH MARTIN
and RALPH BLANE

Moderately slow

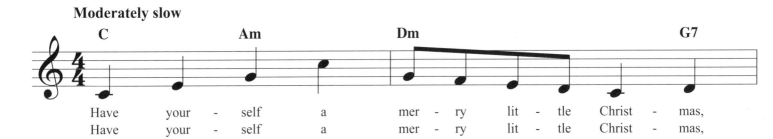

Have your - self a mer - ry lit - tle Christ - mas,
Have your - self a mer - ry lit - tle Christ - mas,

let your heart be light. From now on, our
make the Yule - tide gay. From now on, our

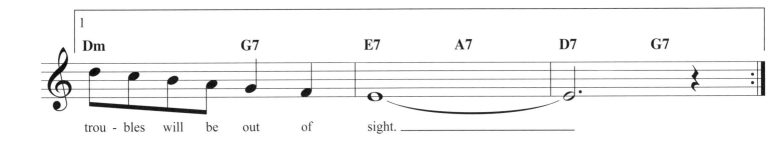

1
trou - bles will be out of sight.

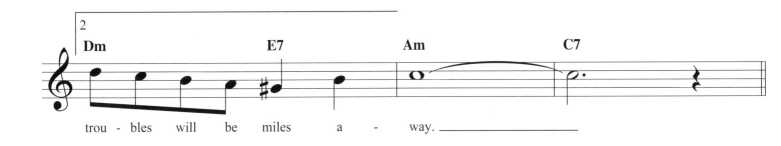

2
trou - bles will be miles a - way.

Here we are as in old - en days, hap - py gold - en days of

yore. Faith - ful friends who are dear to us gath - er

near to us once more. Through the years we

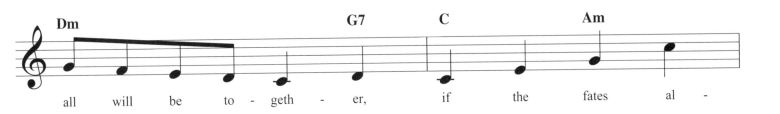

all will be to - geth - er, if the fates al -

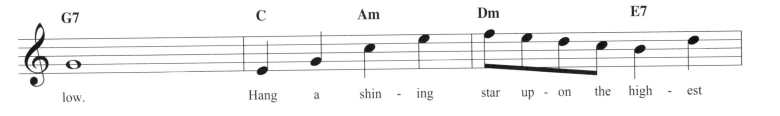

low. Hang a shin - ing star up - on the high - est

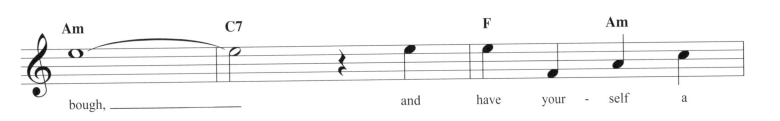

bough, _____ and have your - self a

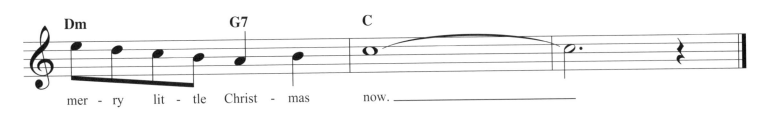

mer - ry lit - tle Christ - mas now. _____

A HOLLY JOLLY CHRISTMAS

Music and Lyrics by
JOHNNY MARKS

I HEARD THE BELLS ON CHRISTMAS DAY

Words by HENRY WADSWORTH LONGFELLOW
Adapted by JOHNNY MARKS
Music by JOHNNY MARKS

Moderately

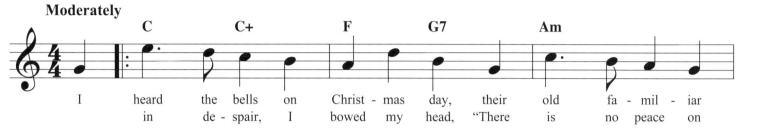

I heard the bells on Christ-mas day, their old fa-mil-iar
in de-spair, I bowed my head, "There is no peace on

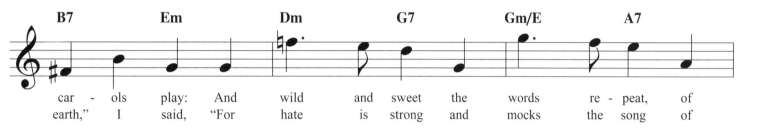

car-ols play: And wild and sweet the words re-peat, of
earth," I said, "For hate is strong and mocks the song of

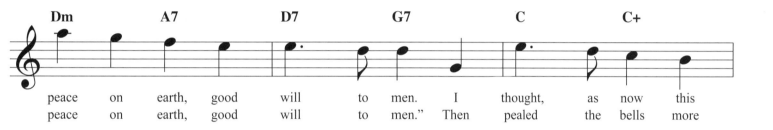

peace on earth, good will to men. I thought, as now this
peace on earth, good will to men." Then pealed the bells more

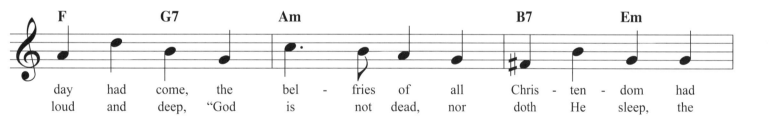

day had come, the bel-fries of all Chris-ten-dom had
loud and deep, "God is not dead, nor doth He sleep, the

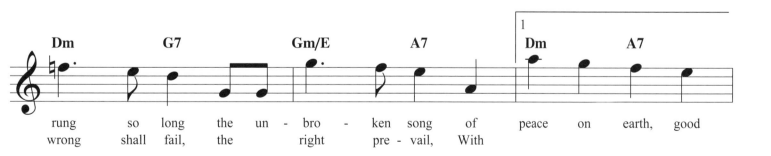

1

rung so long the un-bro-ken song of peace on earth, good
wrong shall fail, the right pre-vail, With

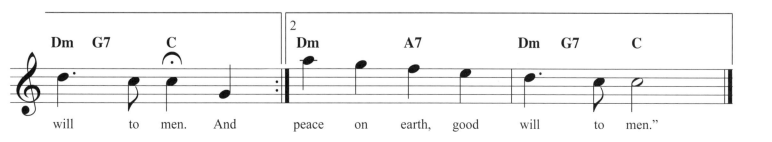

2

will to men. And peace on earth, good will to men."

(There's No Place Like)
HOME FOR THE HOLIDAYS

Words and Music by AL STILLMAN
and ROBERT ALLEN

Moderately

Oh, there's no place like home for the hol - i - days, _____ 'cause no

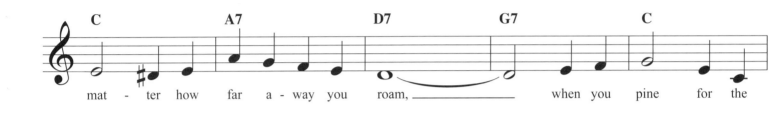

mat - ter how far a - way you roam, _____ when you pine for the

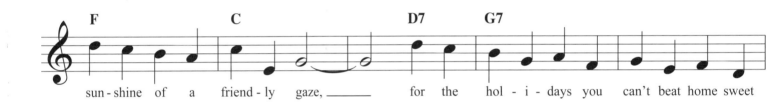

sun - shine of a friend - ly gaze, _____ for the hol - i - days you can't beat home sweet

home. I met a man who lives in Ten - nes - see and he was head - in'

for Penn - syl - va - nia and some home - made pump - kin pie.

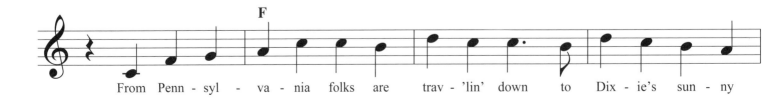

From Penn - syl - va - nia folks are trav - 'lin' down to Dix - ie's sun - ny

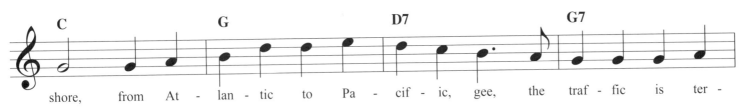

shore, from At - lan - tic to Pa - cif - ic, gee, the traf - fic is ter -

rif - ic. Oh, there's no place like home for the hol - i - days _____

_____ 'cause no mat - ter how far a - way you roam, _____ if you

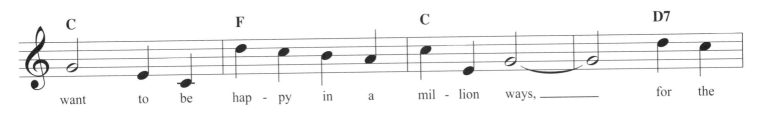

want to be hap - py in a mil - lion ways, _____ for the

1

hol - i - days you can't beat home, sweet home. _____ Oh, there's

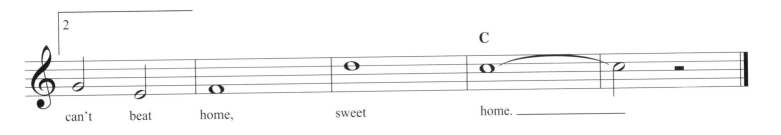

2

can't beat home, sweet home. _____

I SAW MOMMY KISSING SANTA CLAUS

Words and Music by
TOMMIE CONNOR

I'LL BE HOME FOR CHRISTMAS

Words and Music by KIM GANNON
and WALTER KENT

I'll be home for Christ - mas, ____

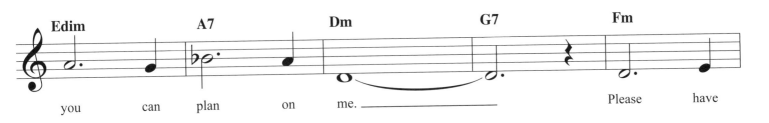

you can plan on me. ____ Please have

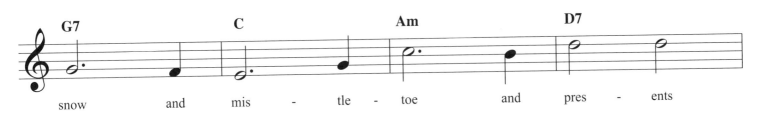

snow and mis - tle - toe and pres - ents

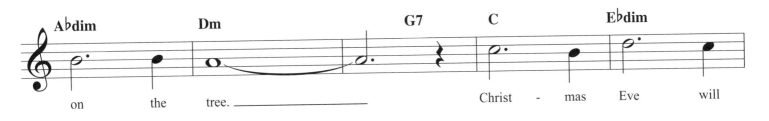

on the tree. ____ Christ - mas Eve will

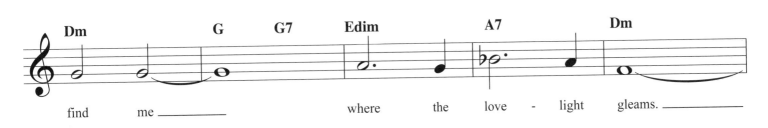

find me ____ where the love - light gleams. ____

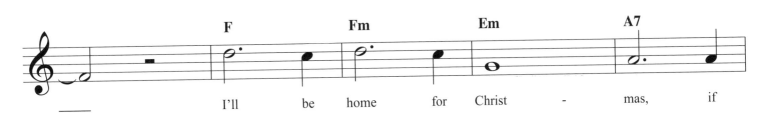

____ I'll be home for Christ - mas, if

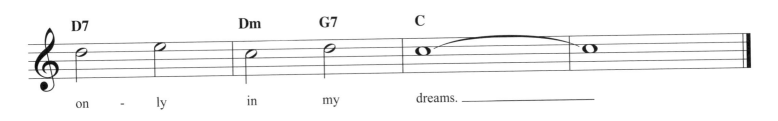

on - ly in my dreams. ____

I WANT A HIPPOPOTAMUS FOR CHRISTMAS
(Hippo the Hero)

Words and Music by
JOHN ROX

Brightly and lightly

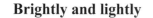

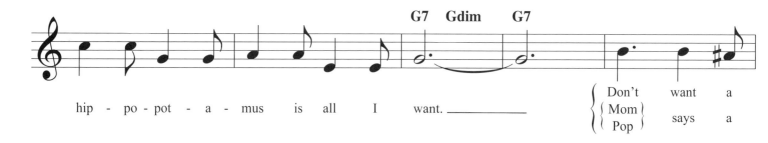

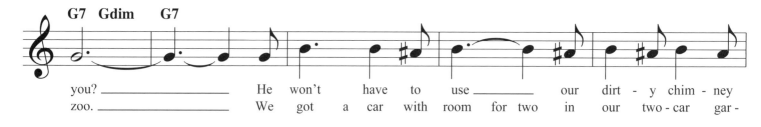

I WONDER AS I WANDER

By JOHN JACOB NILES

Gently

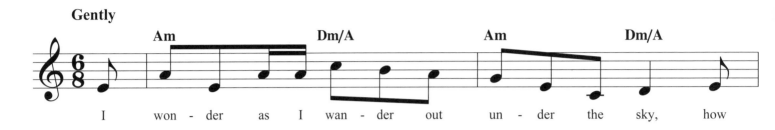

I won - der as I wan - der out un - der the sky, how

Je - sus the Sav - ior did come for to die for poor on - 'ry peo - ple like

you and like I... I won - der as I wan - der out un - der the sky. When

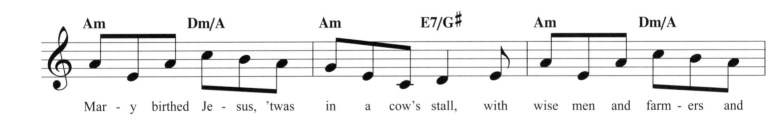

Mar - y birthed Je - sus, 'twas in a cow's stall, with wise men and farm - ers and

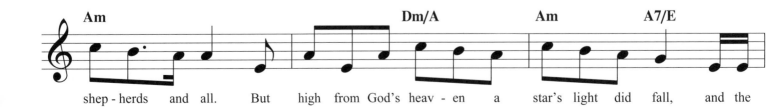

shep - herds and all. But high from God's heav - en a star's light did fall, and the

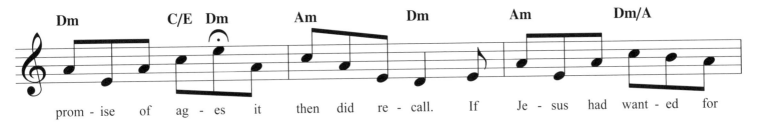

prom - ise of ag - es it then did re - call. If Je - sus had want - ed for

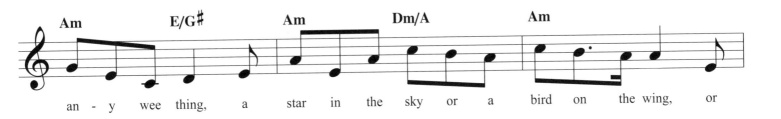

an - y wee thing, a star in the sky or a bird on the wing, or

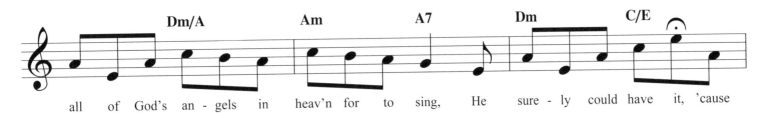

all of God's an - gels in heav'n for to sing, He sure - ly could have it, 'cause

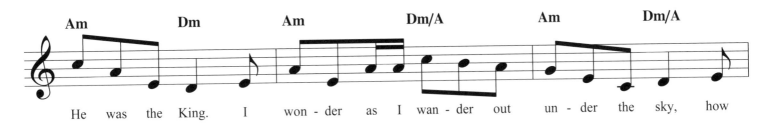

He was the King. I won - der as I wan - der out un - der the sky, how

Je - sus the Sav - ior did come for to die for poor on - 'ry peo - ple like

you and like I... I won - der as I wan - der out un - der the sky.

I'VE GOT MY LOVE TO KEEP ME WARM
from the 20th Century Fox Motion Picture ON THE AVENUE

Words and Music by
IRVING BERLIN

Bright jump tempo

The snow is snow - ing, the wind is
can't re - mem - ber a worse De -

blow - ing, but I can weath - er the storm. ___
cem - ber; just watch those i - ci - cles form. ___

What do I care how
What do I care if

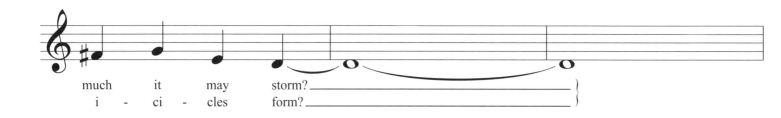

much it may storm? ___
i - ci - cles form? ___

I've got my love to keep me warm. ___

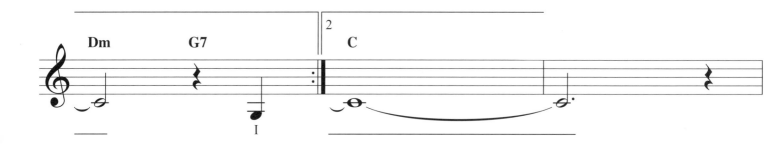

I

IT MUST HAVE BEEN THE MISTLETOE
(Our First Christmas)

Words and Music by JUSTIN WILDE
and DOUG KONECKY

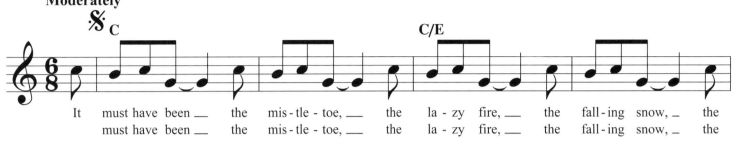

It must have been ___ the mis-tle-toe, ___ the la-zy fire, ___ the fall-ing snow, ___ the
must have been ___ the mis-tle-toe, ___ the la-zy fire, ___ the fall-ing snow, ___ the

mag-ic in ___ the frost-y air, ___ that feel-ing ev-'ry-where. It
mag-ic in ___ the frost-y air, ___ that made me love you. On

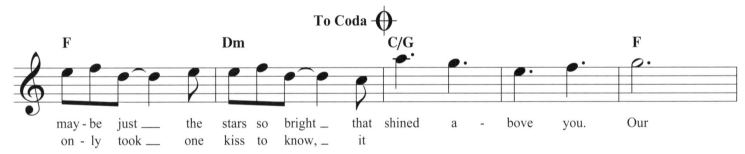

must have been ___ the pret-ty lights ___ that glis-tened ___ in the si-lent night, ___ or
Christ-mas Eve ___ a wish came true, ___ that night I ___ fell in love with you. ___ It

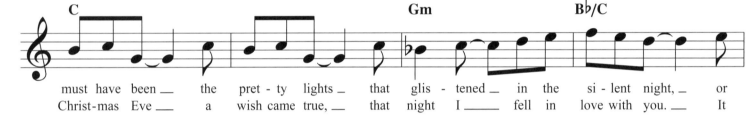

may-be just ___ the stars so bright ___ that shined a - bove you. Our
on-ly took ___ one kiss to know, ___ it

first Christ - mas, more than ___ we'd been dream-ing of. ___

Old Saint Nich - 'las had his fin-gers crossed, ___ that we would fall in love.

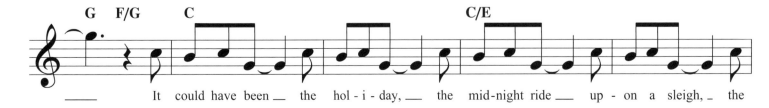

___ It could have been ___ the hol-i-day, ___ the mid-night ride ___ up-on a sleigh, ___ the

IT'S BEGINNING TO LOOK LIKE CHRISTMAS

By MEREDITH WILLSON

It's be - gin - ning to look a lot like Christ - mas,

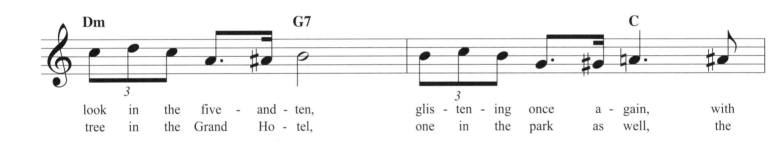

ev - 'ry - where you go. { Take a / There's a

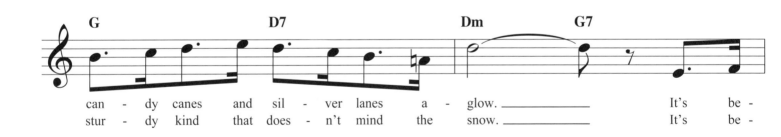

look in the five - and - ten, glis - ten - ing once a - gain, with
tree in the Grand Ho - tel, one in the park as well, the

can - dy canes and sil - ver lanes a - glow. It's be -
stur - dy kind that does - n't mind the snow. It's be -

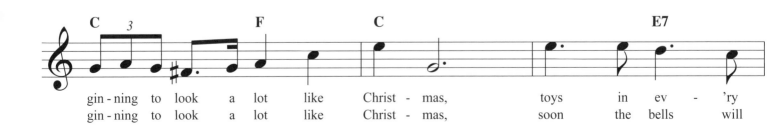

gin - ning to look a lot like Christ - mas, toys in ev - 'ry
gin - ning to look a lot like Christ - mas, soon the bells will

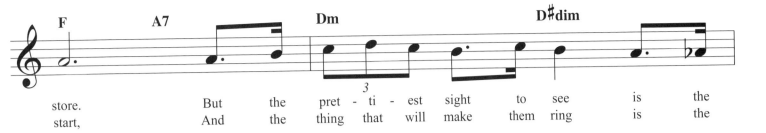

store.   But the pret - ti - est sight to see is the
start,   And the thing that will make them ring is the

To Coda

hol - ly that will be on your own front
car - ol that you sing right with - in your

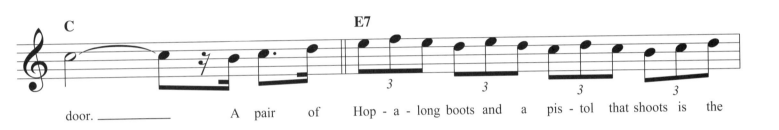

door. _____ A pair of Hop - a - long boots and a pis - tol that shoots is the

wish of Bar - ney and Ben. Dolls that will talk and will go for a walk is the

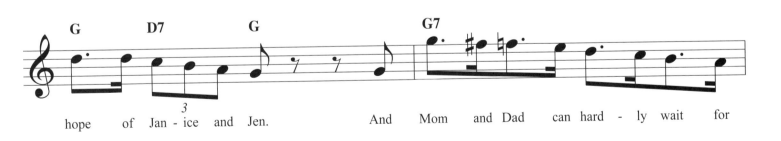

hope of Jan - ice and Jen. And Mom and Dad can hard - ly wait for

D.S. al Coda

school to start a - gain. It's be -

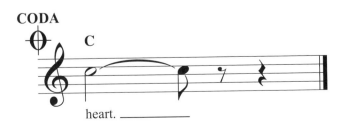

CODA

C

heart. _____

IT'S CHRISTMAS EVERYWHERE

Words and Music by
PAUL ANKA

Moderately slow

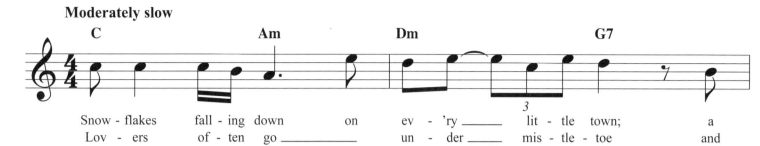

Snow - flakes fall - ing down on ev - 'ry _____ lit - tle town; a
Lov - ers of - ten go _____ un - der _____ mis - tle - toe and

blan - ket of stars a - bove.
kiss un - til dawn's ear - ly light.

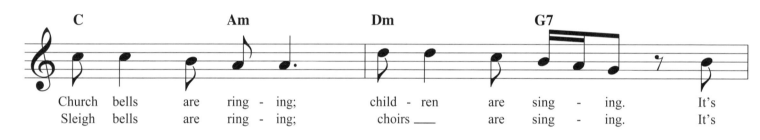

Church bells are ring - ing; child - ren are sing - ing. It's
Sleigh bells are ring - ing; choirs _____ are sing - ing. It's

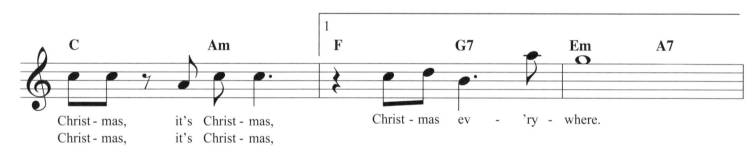

Christ - mas, it's Christ - mas,
Christ - mas, it's Christ - mas,
Christ - mas ev - 'ry - where.

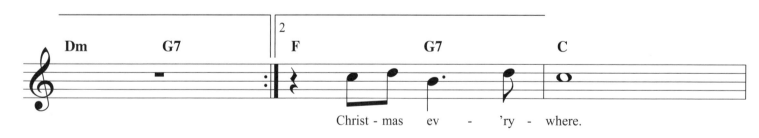

Christ - mas ev - 'ry - where.

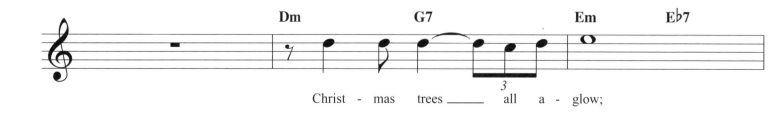

Christ - mas trees _____ all a - glow;

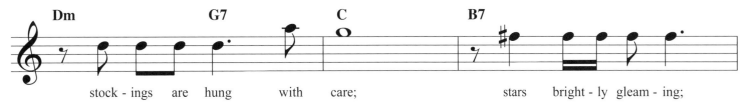

stock - ings are hung with care; stars bright - ly gleam - ing;

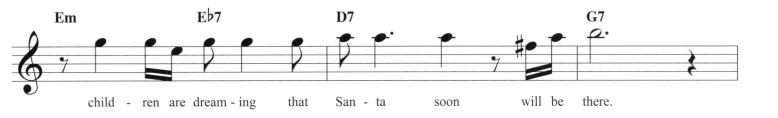

child - ren are dream - ing that San - ta soon will be there.

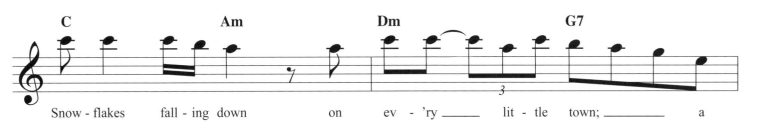

Snow - flakes fall - ing down on ev - 'ry ____ lit - tle town; _____ a

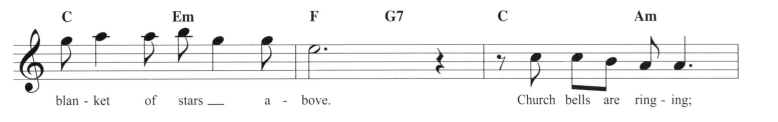

blan - ket of stars ___ a - bove. Church bells are ring - ing;

choirs are sing - ing. It's Christ - mas, it's Christ - mas, Christ - mas ev - 'ry -

where. It's Christ - mas ev - 'ry - where.

IT'S CHRISTMAS IN NEW YORK

Words and Music by
WILLIAM BUTT

JESUS BORN ON THIS DAY

Words and Music by MARIAH CAREY
and WALTER AFANASIEFF

Moderately slow

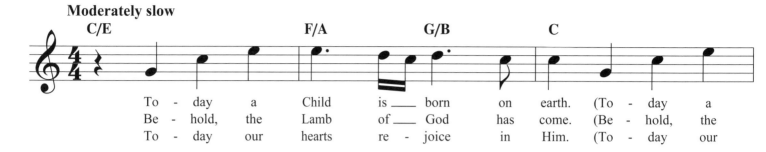

To - day   a   Child   is ___ born   on   earth. (To - day   a
Be - hold,   the   Lamb   of ___ God   has   come. (Be - hold,   the
To - day   our   hearts   re - joice   in   Him. (To - day   our

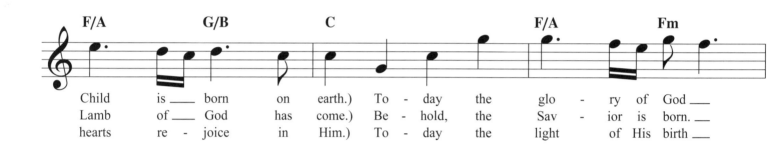

Child   is ___ born   on   earth.)   To - day   the   glo - ry   of   God ___
Lamb   of ___ God   has   come.)   Be - hold,   the   Sav - ior   is   born. ___
hearts   re - joice   in   Him.)   To - day   the   light   of   His   birth ___

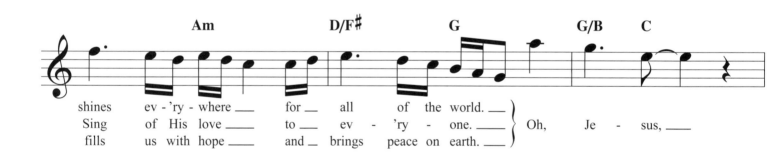

shines   ev - 'ry - where ___ for ___ all   of   the   world. ___
Sing   of   His   love ___ to ___ ev - 'ry - one. ___   Oh,   Je - sus, ___
fills   us   with   hope ___ and ___ brings   peace   on   earth. ___

born   on   this   day, ___   ((1.,3.) He   is   our   light ___ and   sal - va - tion. ___   Oh,
                              ((2.) Heav - en - ly   Child ___ in   a   man - ger. ___   Oh,

Je - sus, ___   born   on   this   day, ___   He   is   the   King ___ of   all   na -
Je - sus, ___   born   on   this   day, ___   He   is   our   Lord ___ and   our   Sav -

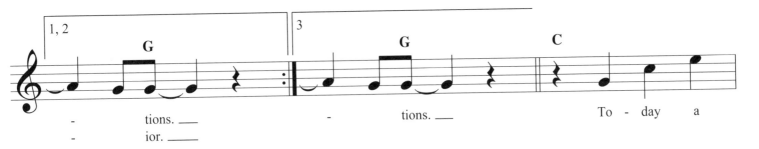

- tions. ___
- ior. ___

Child is ___ born on earth. (To - day a Child is ___ born on

earth.) He is light, He is love, He is grace, born on Christ - mas

day. He is light, He is love, He is grace, born on Christ - mas

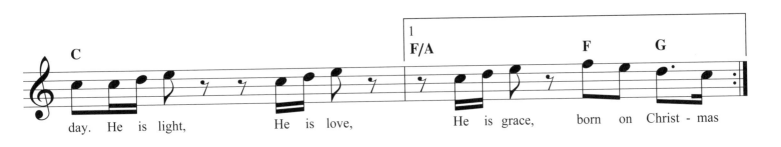

day. He is light, He is love, He is grace, born on Christ - mas

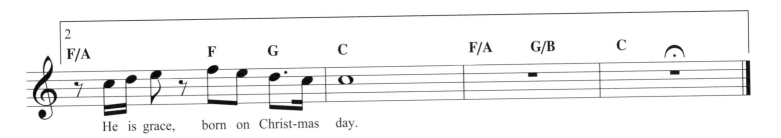

He is grace, born on Christ-mas day.

JINGLE BELL ROCK

Words and Music by JOE BEAL
and JIM BOOTHE

Moderately

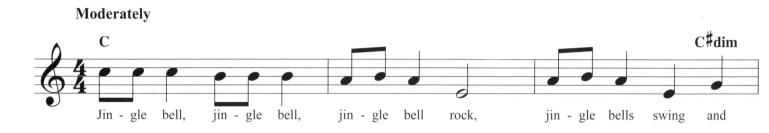

Jin - gle bell, jin - gle bell, jin - gle bell rock, jin - gle bells swing and

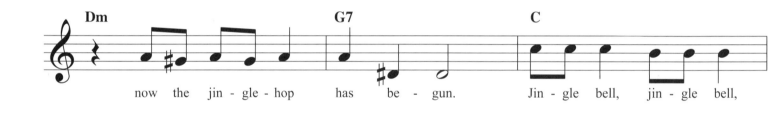

jin - gle bells ring. Snow - in' and blow - in' up bush - els of fun,

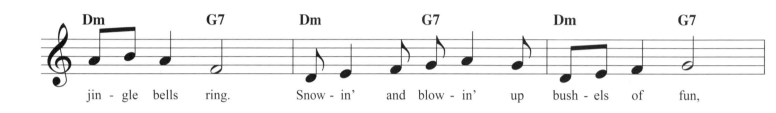

now the jin - gle-hop has be - gun. Jin - gle bell, jin - gle bell,

jin - gle bell rock, jin - gle bells chime in jin - gle bell time,

danc - in' and pranc - in' in Jin - gle Bell Square in the frost - y

air. What a bright __ time, __ it's the right __ time __ to

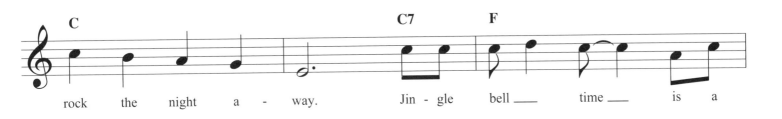

rock the night a - way. Jin - gle bell __ time __ is a

swell time __ to go glid - in' in a one - horse sleigh.

Gid - dy - up, jin - gle horse, pick up your feet. Jin - gle a - round the clock.

Mix and min - gle in a jin - gl - in' beat, that's the jin - gle bell

rock. that's the jin - gle bell, that's the jin - gle bell rock.

Last Christmas

Words and Music by
GEORGE MICHAEL

Slowly and freely

Last Christ - mas I gave you my heart, __ but the ver - y next day you

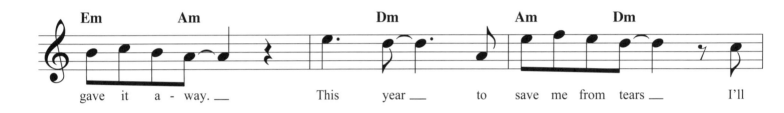

gave it a - way. __ This year __ to save me from tears __ I'll

give it to some - one spe - cial. Last Christ - mas I

gave you my heart, __ but the ver - y next day you gave it a - way. __

This year __ to save me from tears __ I'll give it to some - one spe -

- cial. *(Instrumental)*

CODA

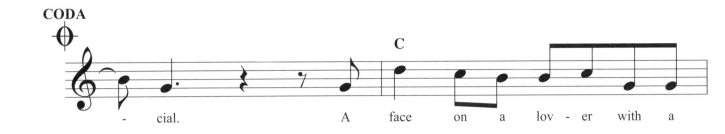

-cial. A face on a lov-er with a

fire in his heart, _ a man un-der cov-er but you tore him a-part. _

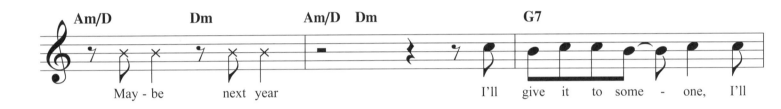

May-be next year I'll give it to some - one, I'll

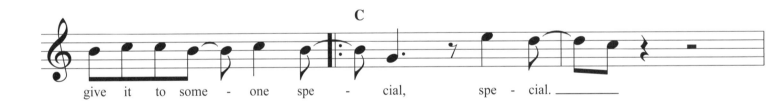

give it to some - one spe - cial, spe - cial. _____

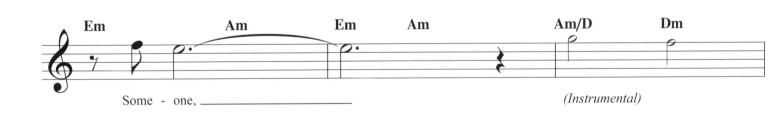

Some - one, _____ (Instrumental)

Repeat ad lib. and Fade

some-one. I'll give it to some - one, I'll give it to some - one spe-

LET IT SNOW! LET IT SNOW! LET IT SNOW!

Words by SAMMY CAHN
Music by JULE STYNE

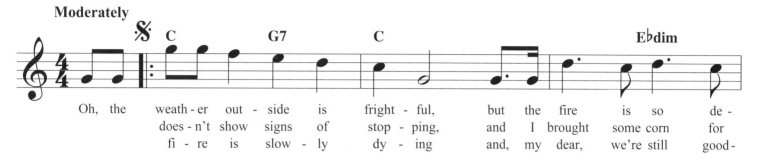

Oh, the weath-er out-side is fright-ful, but the fire is so de-
does-n't show signs of stop-ping, and I brought some corn for
fi-re is slow-ly dy-ing and, my dear, we're still good-

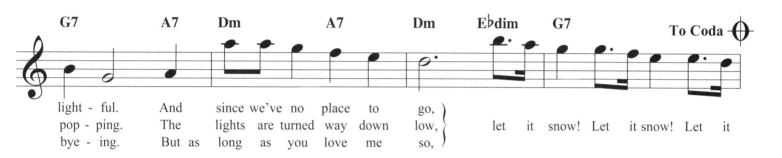

light-ful. And since we've no place to go,
pop-ping. The lights are turned way down low,   let it snow! Let it snow! Let it
bye-ing. But as long as you love me so,

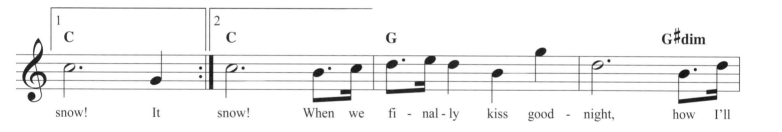

snow!   It snow!   When we fi-nal-ly kiss good-night,   how I'll

hate go-ing out in the storm.   But if you real-ly hold me tight,

all the way home I'll be warm.   The

snow!

THE LITTLE DRUMMER BOY

Words and Music by HARRY SIMEONE,
HENRY ONORATI and KATHERINE DAVIS

MARY'S LITTLE BOY CHILD

Words and Music by
JESTER HAIRSTON

LITTLE SAINT NICK

Words and Music by BRIAN WILSON
and MIKE LOVE

Well, _____ way up north where the air gets cold, ___ there's a
lit - tle bob - sled, we call it Old Saint Nick, ___ but she'll
haul - in' through the snow at a fright - 'nin' speed ___ with a

tale a - bout Christ - mas that you've all been told. _____ And a
walk a to - bog - gan with a four - speed stick. ___ She's
half a doz - en deer _____ with _____ Ru - dy to lead. He's

real fa - mous cat all dressed up in red, _____ and he
can - dy ap - ple red with a ski for a wheel, and when
got - ta wear his gog - gles 'cause the snow real - ly flies, and he's

spends the whole ___ year work - in' out on his sled. ___
San - ta hits the gas, man, just watch her _____ peel. ___ } It's the
cruis - in' ev - 'ry pad with a lit - tle sur - prise. ___

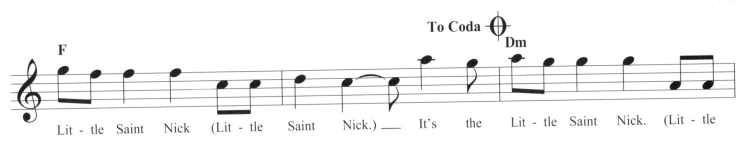

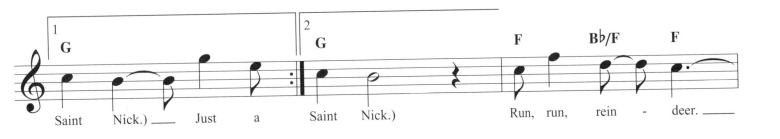

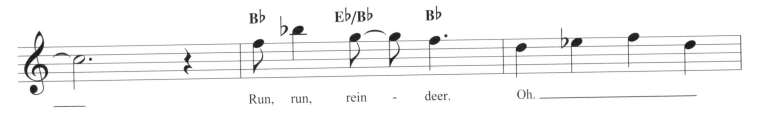

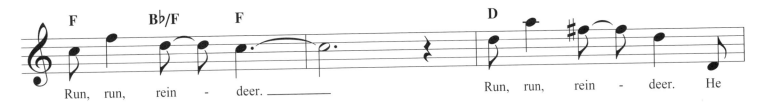

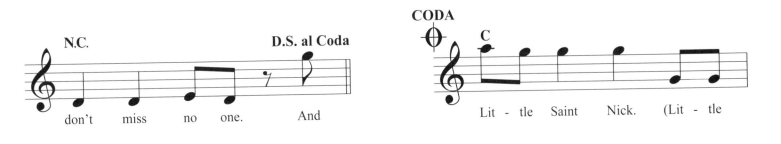

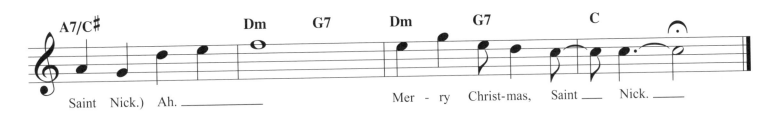

A MARSHMALLOW WORLD

Words by CARL SIGMAN
Music by PETER DE ROSE

With motion

It's a marsh - mal - low world in the win - ter_____ when the
marsh - mal - low clouds be - ing friend - ly_____ in the

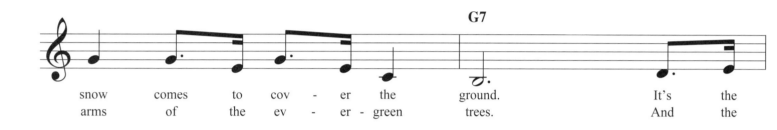

snow comes to cov - er the ground. It's the
arms of the ev - er - green trees. And the

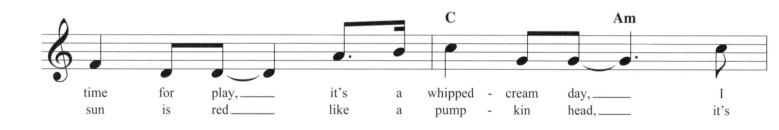

time for play,_____ it's a whipped - cream day,_____ I
sun is red_____ like a pump - kin head,_____ it's

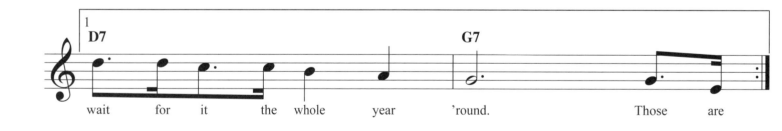

wait for it the whole year 'round. Those are

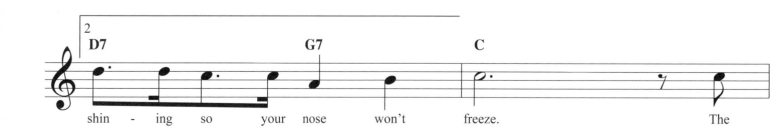

shin - ing so your nose won't freeze. The

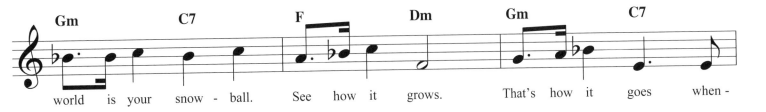

world is your snow - ball. See how it grows. That's how it goes when -

ev - er it snows. The world is your snow - ball

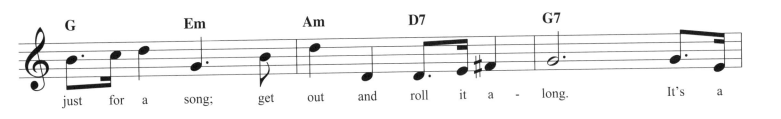

just for a song; get out and roll it a - long. It's a

yum - yum - my world made for sweet - hearts. _____ Take a

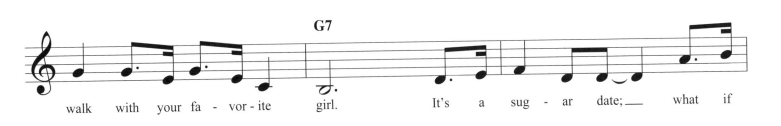

walk with your fa - vor - ite girl. It's a sug - ar date; __ what if

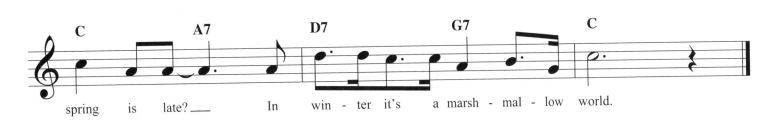

spring is late? __ In win - ter it's a marsh - mal - low world.

MARY, DID YOU KNOW?

Words and Music by MARK LOWRY
and BUDDY GREENE

MELE KALIKIMAKA

Words and Music by
R. ALEX ANDERSON

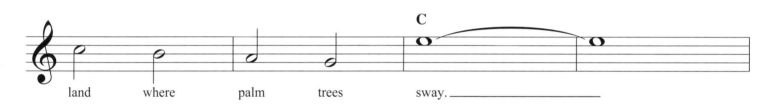

MISTER SANTA

Words and Music by
PAT BALLARD

1. Mis - ter San - ta,
2., 3. (See additional verses)
bring {me/us} some toys _____ bring Mer - ry
Christ - mas to all girls and boys. _____ And ev - 'ry night {I'll/we'll}
go to sleep sing - ing and dream a - bout the pres - ents you'll be
bring - ing. San - ta, prom - ise {me/us} please, _____ give ev - 'ry
rein - deer a hug and a squeeze. _ {I'll/we'll} be good, _____ as good can be, _____
_____ Mis - ter San - ta don't for - get me. _____ Mis - ter

Additional Verses

2. Mister Santa, dear old Saint Nick
   Be awful careful and please don't get sick
   Put on your coat when breezes are blowin'
   And when you cross the street look where you're goin'.
   Santa, we (I) love you so,
   We (I) hope you never get lost in the snow.
   Take your time when you unpack,
   Mister Santa don't hurry back.

3. Mister Santa, we've been so good
   We've washed the dishes and done what we should.
   Made up the beds and scrubbed up our toesies,
   We've used a kleenex when we've blown our nosies.
   Santa look at our ears, they're clean as whistles,
   We're sharper than shears
   Now we've put you on the spot,
   Mister Santa bring us a lot.

MERRY CHRISTMAS, DARLING

Words and Music by RICHARD CARPENTER
and FRANK POOLER

Moderately

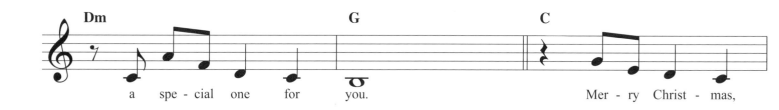

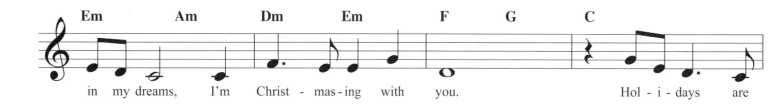

you.   The ___ lights on my tree   I   wish   you   could   see,

I   wish it   ev - 'ry   day.   The logs   on   the   fire ___

fill me with de - sire   to   see   you   and   to ___ say   that I

wish   you   mer -   ry   Christ - mas,   hap - py   New   Year

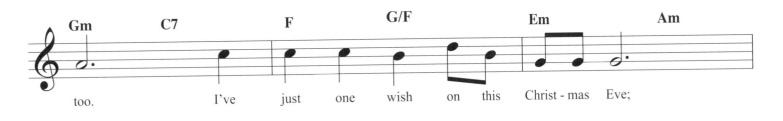

too.   I've   just   one   wish   on   this   Christ - mas   Eve;

I   wish   I   were   with   you.   The ___   I   wish   I   were   with

you.   I   wish   I   were   with   you.

MERRY, MERRY CHRISTMAS BABY

Words and Music by GILBERT LOPEZ
and MARGO SYLVIA

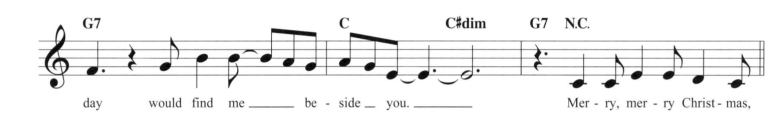

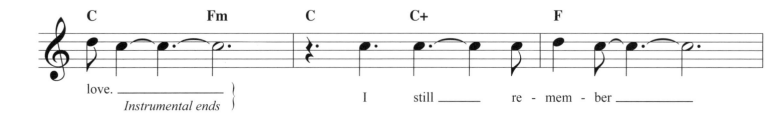

the gifts we gave ____ to each oth - er. ____ This love I

hold ____ with - in my heart ____

still grows, though we're ____ a - part. Have a mer - ry Christ - mas,

ba - by, ____ and a hap - py ____ New Year too. ____

I am hop - ing that you'll find a ____ love as ____ true as mine. Mer - ry, mer - ry Christ - mas,

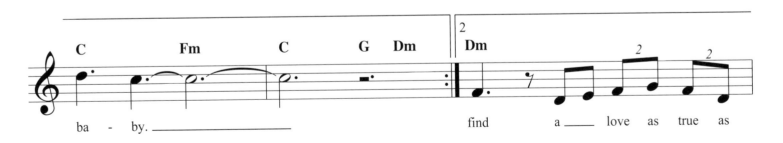

ba - by. ____ find a ____ love as true as

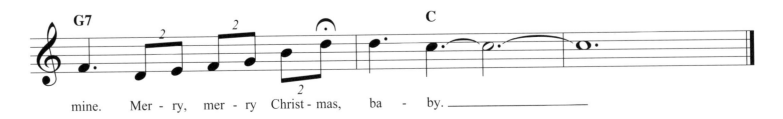

mine. Mer - ry, mer - ry Christ - mas, ba - by. ____

MISS YOU MOST AT CHRISTMAS TIME

Words and Music by MARIAH CAREY
and WALTER AFANASIEFF

SAME OLD LANG SYNE

Words and Music by
DAN FOGELBERG

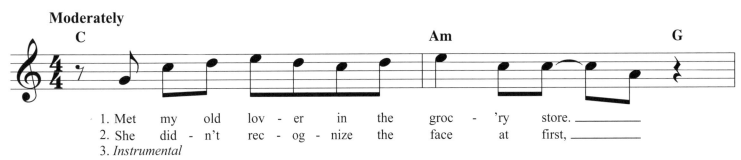

1. Met my old lov - er in the groc - 'ry store. _____
2. She did - n't rec - og - nize the face at first, _____
3. *Instrumental*
4.-8. *See additional lyrics*

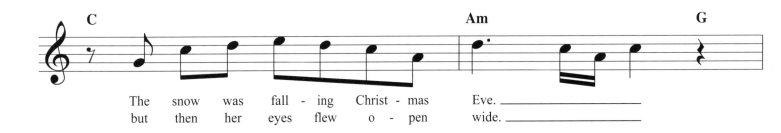

The snow was fall - ing Christ - mas Eve. _____
but then her eyes flew o - pen wide. _____

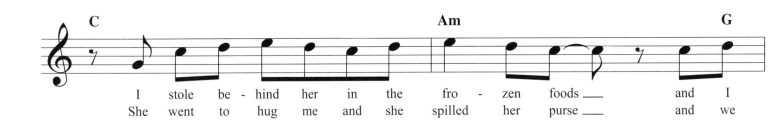

I stole be - hind her in the fro - zen foods __ and I
She went to hug me and she spilled her purse __ and we

touched her on __ the sleeve. _____
laughed un - til __ we cried. _____

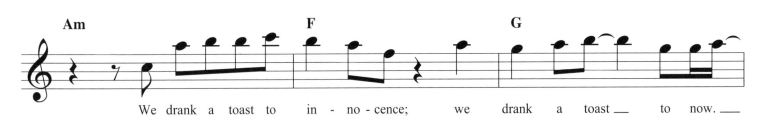

We drank a toast to in - no - cence; we drank a toast __ to now. __

___ We tried to reach be - yond the emp - ti - ness, but

pain. _____ And, as I turned to make my way ___ back ___ home, the

snow turned in - to rain... *(Instrumental ad lib.)*

Additional Lyrics

4. We took her groc'ries to the checkout stand;
The food was totalled up and bagged.
We stood there, lost in our embarrassment,
As the conversation lagged.

5. We went to have ourselves a drink or two,
But couldn't find an open bar.
We bought a six-pack at the liquor store
And we drank it in her car.

6. She said she's married her an architect,
Who kept her warm and safe and dry.
She would have like to say she loved the man,
But she didn't like to lie.

7. I said the years had been a friend to her
And that her eyes were still as blue.
But in those eyes I wasn't sure if I
Saw doubt or gratitude.

8. She said she saw me in the record stores,
And that I must be doing well.
I said the audience was heavenly,
But the traveling was hell.

MISTLETOE AND HOLLY

Words and Music by FRANK SINATRA,
DOK STANFORD and HENRY W. SANICOLA

Medium Bounce

Oh, by gosh, by gol - ly, it's time for mis - tle - toe and hol - ly,_____
Oh, by gosh, by jin - gle, it's time for car - ols and Kris Krin - gle,_____
Oh, by gosh, by gol - ly, it's time for mis - tle - toe and hol - ly,_____

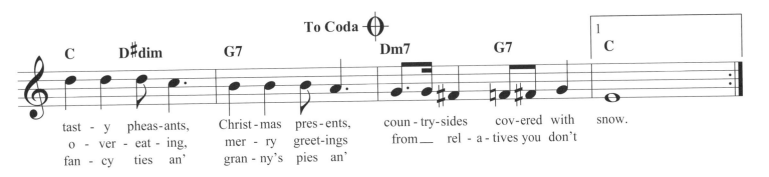

tast - y pheas - ants, Christ - mas pres - ents, coun - try - sides cov - ered with snow.
o - ver - eat - ing, mer - ry greet - ings from___ rel - a - tives you don't
fan - cy ties an' gran - ny's pies an'

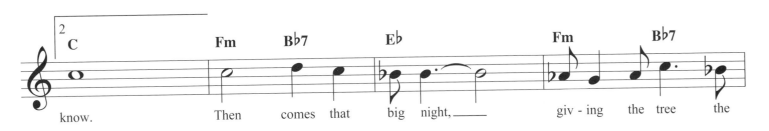

know. Then comes that big night,_____ giv - ing the tree the

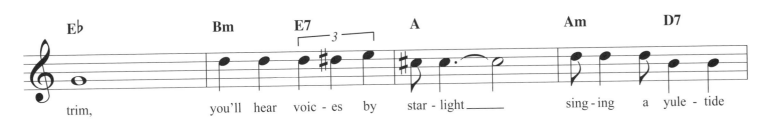

trim, you'll hear voic - es by star - light_____ sing - ing a yule - tide

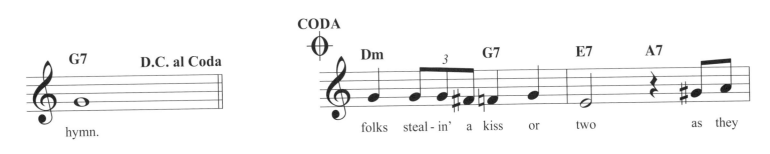

hymn.   **D.C. al Coda**

CODA

folks steal - in' a kiss or two as they

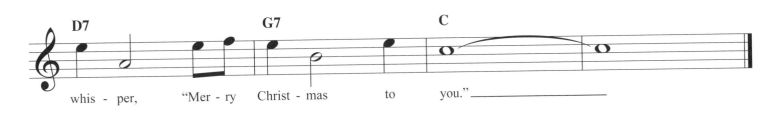

whis - per, "Mer - ry Christ - mas to you."_____

THE MOST WONDERFUL TIME OF THE YEAR

Words and Music by EDDIE POLA
and GEORGE WYLE

Brightly, in one

It's the most   won-der-ful time _____ of the
hap - hap-pi-est sea - son of
most   won-der-ful time _____ of the

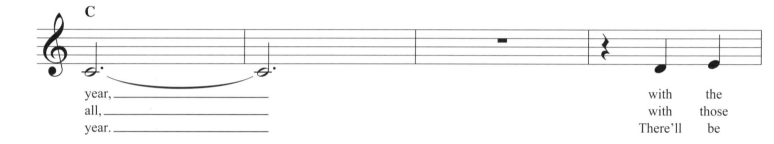

year, _____ with the
all, _____ with those
year. _____ There'll be

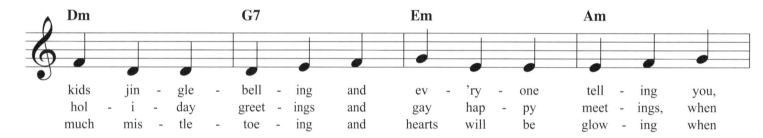

kids jin - gle - bell - ing and ev - 'ry - one tell - ing you,
hol - i - day greet - ings and gay hap - py meet - ings, when
much mis - tle - toe - ing and hearts will be glow - ing when

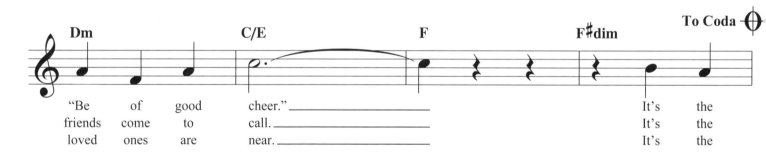

"Be of good cheer." _____ It's the
friends come to call. _____ It's the
loved ones are near. _____ It's the

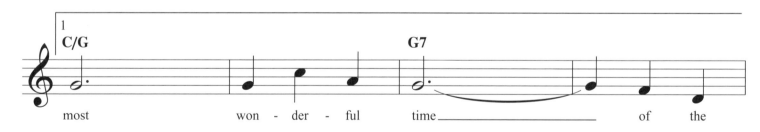

most   won - der - ful time _____ of the

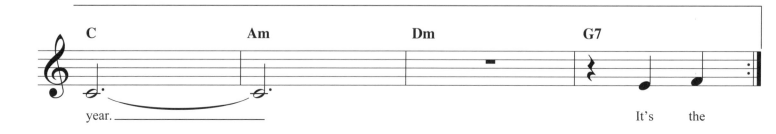

year. _____ It's the

MY FAVORITE THINGS
from THE SOUND OF MUSIC

Lyrics by OSCAR HAMMERSTEIN II
Music by RICHARD RODGERS

Moderately

Rain - drops on ros - es and whis - kers on kit - tens,
Cream - col - ored po - nies and crisp ap - ple strud - els,

bright cop - per ket - tles and warm wool - en mit - tens,
door - bells and sleigh - bells and schnitz - el with noo - dles,

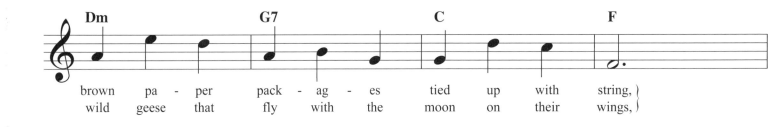

brown pa - per pack - ag - es tied up with string,
wild geese that fly with the moon on their wings,

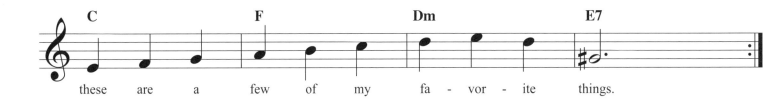

these are a few of my fa - vor - ite things.

Girls in white dress - es with blue sat - in sash - es,

snow - flakes that stay on my nose and eye - lash - es,

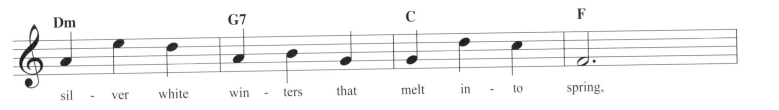

sil - ver   white   win - ters   that   melt   in - to   spring,

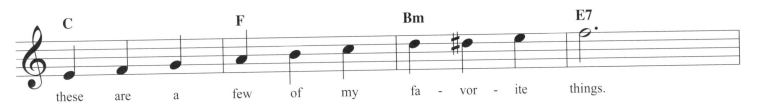

these   are   a   few   of   my   fa - vor - ite   things.

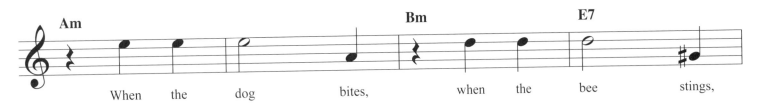

When   the   dog   bites,   when   the   bee   stings,

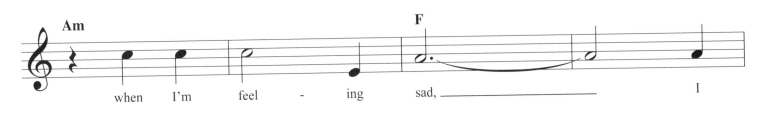

when   I'm   feel - ing   sad, _____   I

sim - ply   re - mem - ber   my   fa - vor - ite   things   and

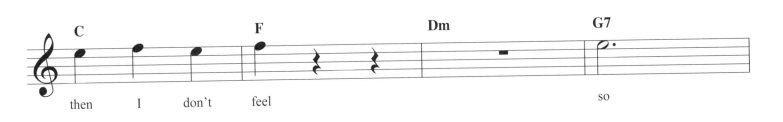

then   I   don't   feel   so

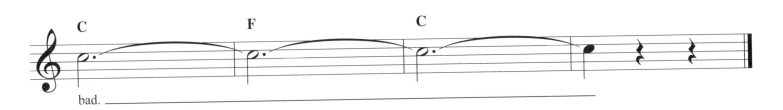

bad. _____

THE NIGHT BEFORE CHRISTMAS SONG

Music by JOHNNY MARKS
Lyrics adapted by JOHNNY MARKS
from CLEMENT MOORE'S Poem

Gaily

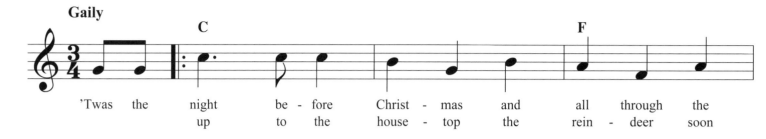

'Twas the night be - fore Christ - mas and all through the
up to the house - top the rein - deer soon

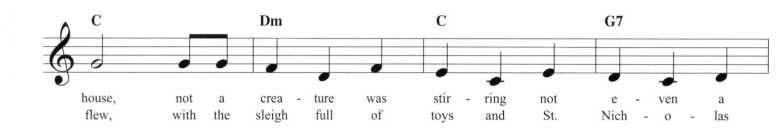

house, not a crea - ture was stir - ring not e - ven a
flew, with the sleigh full of toys and St. Nich - o - las

mouse. All the stock - ings were hung by the chim - ney with
too. Down the chim - ney he came with a leap and a

care, in the hope that Saint Nich - o - las soon would be
bound. He was dressed all in fur and his bel - ly was

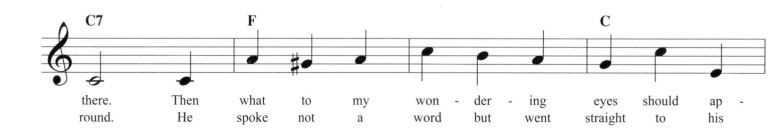

there. Then what to my won - der - ing eyes should ap -
round. He spoke not a word but went straight to his

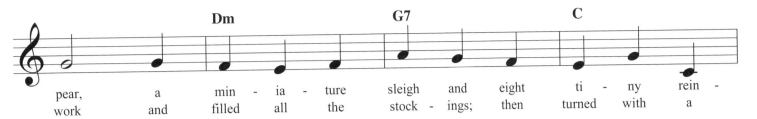

pear,   a   min - ia - ture   sleigh and   eight   ti - ny   rein -
work   and   filled   all   the   stock - ings;   then   turned   with   a

deer.   A   lit - tle   old   driv - er   so   live - ly   and   quick,   I
jerk.   And   lay - ing   his   fin - ger   a - side   of   his   nose,   then

knew   in   a   mo - ment   it   must   be   Saint   Nick.   And   more
giv - ing   a   nod   up   the   chim - ney   he   rose;   but   I

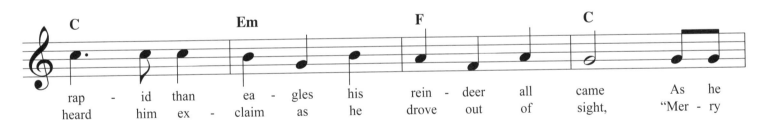

rap - id   than   ea - gles   his   rein - deer   all   came,   As   he
heard   him   ex - claim   as   he   drove   out   of   sight,   "Mer - ry

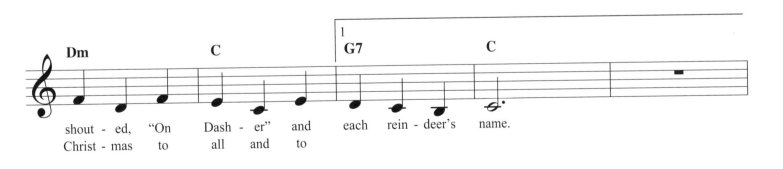

shout - ed,   "On   Dash - er"   and   each   rein - deer's   name.
Christ - mas   to   all   and   to

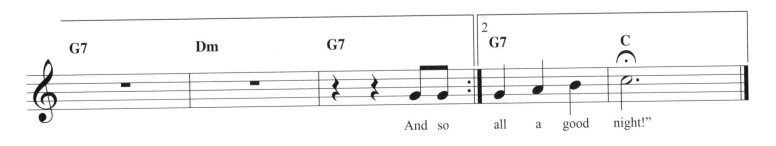

And   so   all   a   good   night!"

NOT THAT FAR FROM BETHLEHEM

Words and Music by JEFF BORDERS,
GAYLA BORDERS and LOWELL ALEXANDER

NUTTIN' FOR CHRISTMAS

Words and Music by ROY C. BENNETT
and SID TEPPER

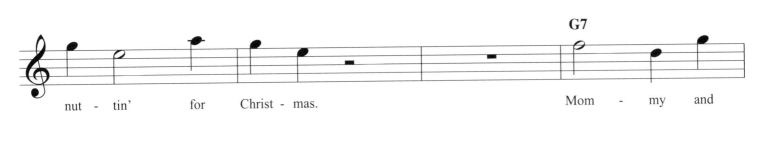

nut - tin' for Christ - mas. Mom - my and

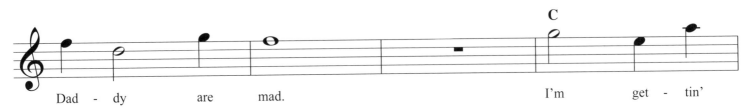

Dad - dy are mad. I'm get - tin'

nut - tin' for Christ - mas, 'cause I ain't been

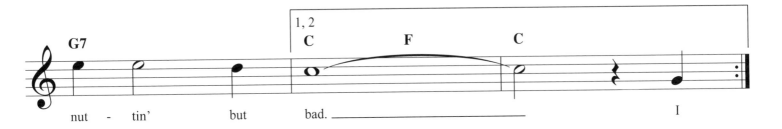

nut - tin' but bad. I

bad. So, you bet - ter be good, what -

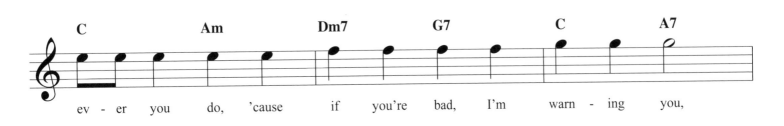

ev - er you do, 'cause if you're bad, I'm warn - ing you,

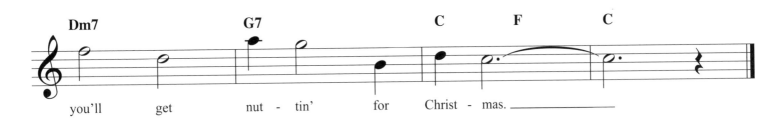

you'll get nut - tin' for Christ - mas.

OLD TOY TRAINS

Words and Music by
ROGER MILLER

Moderately

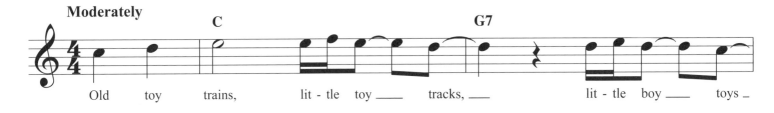

Old toy trains, lit - tle toy ____ tracks, ____ lit - tle boy ____ toys ____

____ com - in' from a sack, car - ried by a man dressed in white and

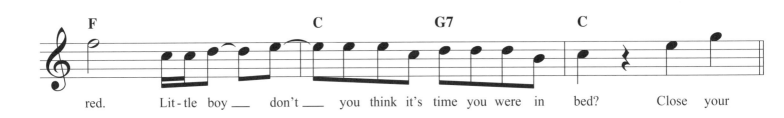

red. Lit - tle boy ____ don't ____ you think it's time you were in bed? Close your

eyes, _____ lis - ten to the skies. _____

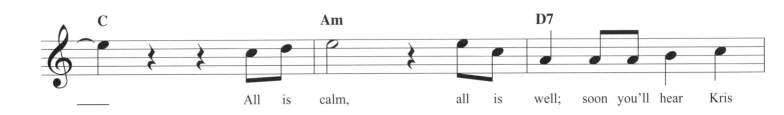

____ All is calm, all is well; soon you'll hear Kris

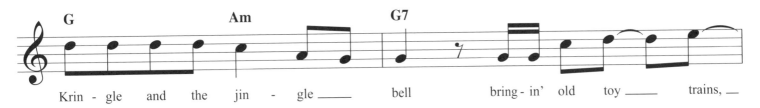

Krin - gle and the jin - gle ___ bell bring-in' old toy ___ trains, ___

___ lit - tle toy ___ tracks, ___ lit - tle boy ___ toys ___

___ com - in' from a sack, car - ried by a man dressed in white and

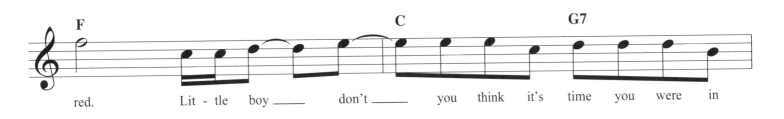

red. Lit - tle boy ___ don't ___ you think it's time you were in

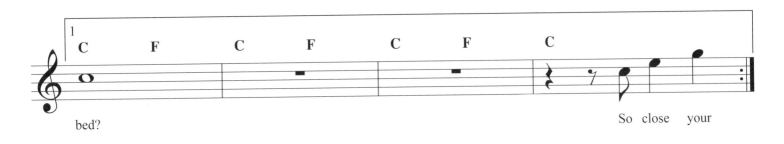

bed? So close your

bed? Lit - tle boy ___ don't ___ you think it's time you were in bed?

ONE LITTLE CHRISTMAS TREE

Words and Music by RONALD N. MILLER
and BRYAN WELLS

PLEASE COME HOME FOR CHRISTMAS

Words and Music by CHARLES BROWN
and GENE REDD

PRETTY PAPER

Words and Music by
WILLIE NELSON

Crowd-ed streets, bus-y feet hus-tle by you; ____ Down-town

shop-pers Christ-mas is nigh. ____ There he

sits all a-lone on the side-walk, ____

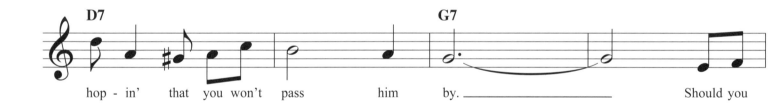

hop-in' that you won't pass him by. ____ Should you

stop; bet-ter not, much too bus-y; ____ you'd bet-ter

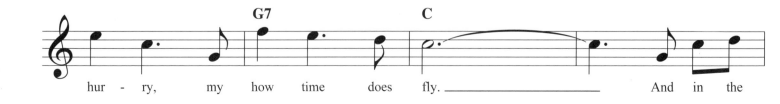

hur-ry, my how time does fly. ____ And in the

dis - tance the ring - ing of ___ laugh - ter, _____ and in the

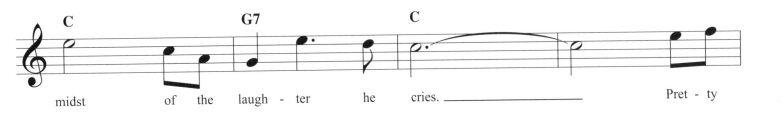

midst of the laugh - ter he cries. _____ Pret - ty

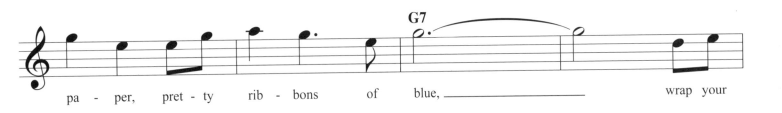

pa - per, pret - ty rib - bons of blue, _____ wrap your

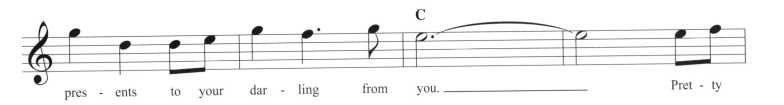

pres - ents to your dar - ling from you. _____ Pret - ty

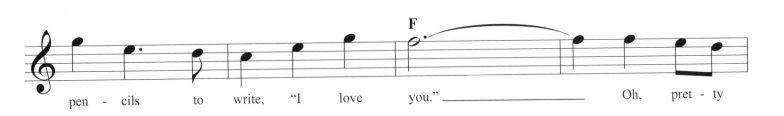

pen - cils to write, "I love you." _____ Oh, pret - ty

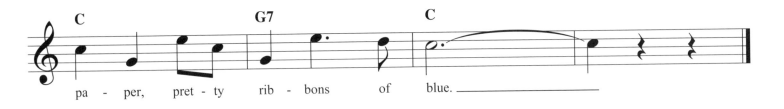

pa - per, pret - ty rib - bons of blue. _____

ROCKIN' AROUND THE CHRISTMAS TREE

Music and Lyrics by
JOHNNY MARKS

Lively

Rock - in' a - round the Christ - mas tree ___ at the Christ - mas par - ty hop, ___

___ Mis - tle - toe hung where you can see ___ ev - 'ry

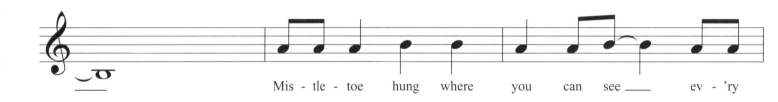

cou - ple tries to stop. Rock - in' a - round the

Christ - mas tree, ___ let the Christ - mas spir - it ring. ___

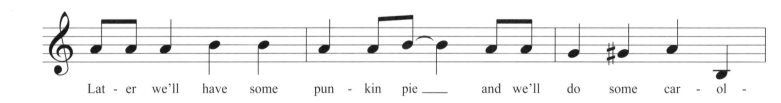

Lat - er we'll have some pun - kin pie ___ and we'll do some car - ol -

ing. You will get a sen - ti - men - tal

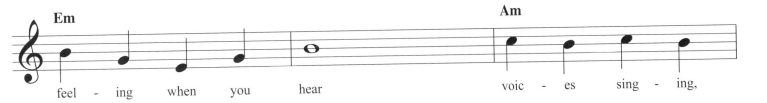

feel - ing when you hear voic - es sing - ing,

"Let's be jol - ly. Deck the halls with boughs of hol - ly."

Rock - in' a - round the Christ - mas tree. ___ Have a hap - py hol - i - day. ___

___ Ev - 'ry - one danc - ing mer - ri - ly ___ in the

new old fash - ioned way. new old

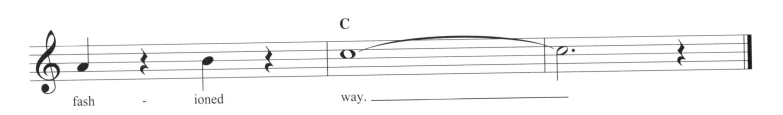

fash - ioned way. ___

RUDOLPH THE RED-NOSED REINDEER

Music and Lyrics by
JOHNNY MARKS

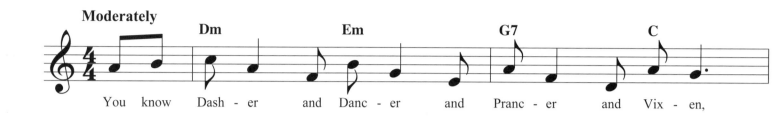

You know Dash - er and Danc - er and Pranc - er and Vix - en,

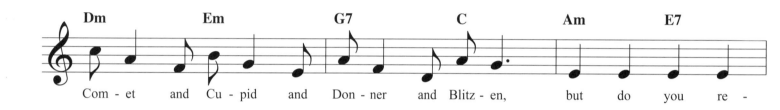

Com - et and Cu - pid and Don - ner and Blitz - en, but do you re -

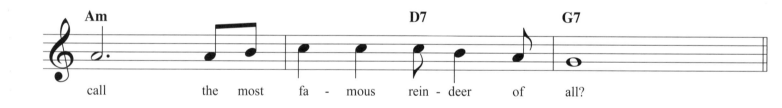

call the most fa - mous rein - deer of all?

Ru - dolph the red - nosed rein - deer had a ver - y shin - y
All of the oth - er rein - deer used to laugh and call him

nose, and if you ev - er saw it,
names, they nev - er let poor Ru - dolph

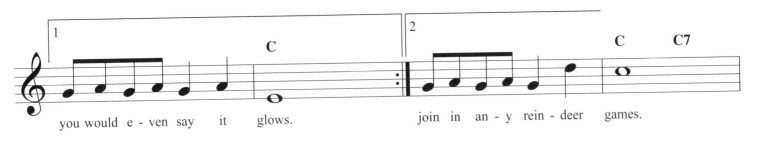

you would e - ven say it glows.   join in an - y rein - deer games.

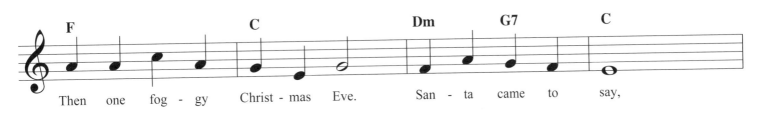

Then one fog - gy Christ - mas Eve.   San - ta came to say,

"Ru - dolph, with your nose so bright,   won't you guide my sleigh to - night?" _

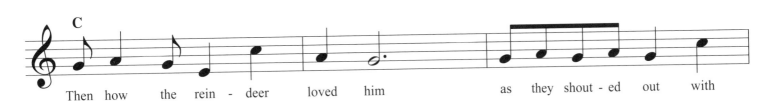

Then how the rein - deer loved him   as they shout - ed out with

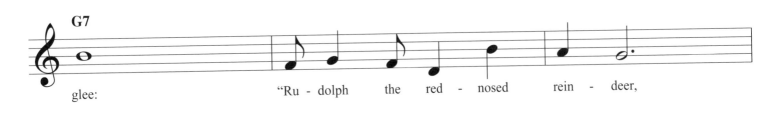

glee: "Ru - dolph the red - nosed rein - deer,

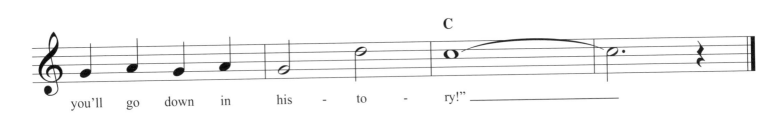

you'll go down in his - to - ry!" _____

SANTA BABY

By JOAN JAVITS, PHIL SPRINGER
and TONY SPRINGER

Moderately

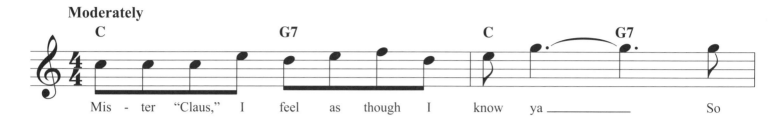

Mis- ter "Claus," I feel as though I know ya _____ So

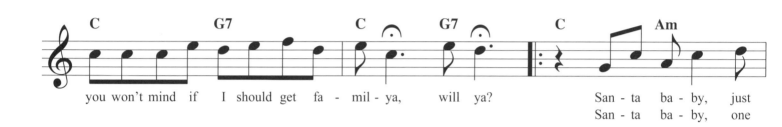

you won't mind if I should get fa - mil- ya, will ya?
San- ta ba - by, just
San- ta ba - by, one

slip a sa- ble un- der the tree _____ for me. __ Been an aw- ful good girl, __
lit- tle thing I real- ly do need: __ the deed __ to a plat- i- num mine. _

_____ San- ta ba - by. So hur- ry down the chim- ney to - night. _____
_____ San- ta hon- ey. So hur- ry down the chim- ney to - night. _____

_____ San- ta ba - by, a fif- ty- four con- vert- i- ble, too,
_____ San- ta cu- tie, and fill my stock- ing with a du- plex

_____ light blue. __ I'll wait up for you, dear _____ San- ta ba - by, so
_____ and cheques. _ Sign your X on the line, _____ San- ta cu- tie, and

153

SANTA CLAUS IS COMIN' TO TOWN

Words by HAVEN GILLESPIE
Music by J. FRED COOTS

SILVER AND GOLD

Music and Lyrics by
JOHNNY MARKS

SHAKE ME I RATTLE
(Squeeze Me I Cry)

Words and Music by HAL HACKADY
and CHARLES NAYLOR

Moderately slow

I was pass - ing by a toy shop on the
called an - oth - er toy shop on a
late and snow was fall - ing as the

cor - ner of the square, where a lit - tle girl was
square so long a - go, where I saw a lit - tle
shop - pers hur - ried by past the girl - ie at the

look - ing in the win - dow there. She was
dol - ly that I want - ed so. I re -
win - dow with her lit - tle head held high. They were

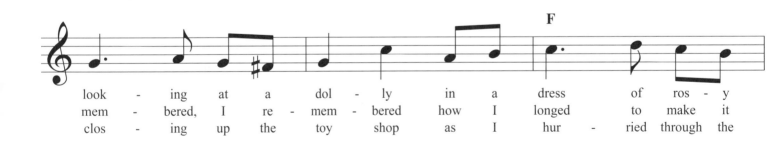

look - ing at a dol - ly in a dress of ros - y
mem - bered, I re - mem - bered how I longed to make it
clos - ing up the toy shop as I hur - ried through the

red, and a - round the pret - ty dol - ly hung a
mine, and a - round that oth - er dol - ly hung an -
door, just in time to buy the dol - ly that her

lit - tle sign that said: Shake me, I
oth - er lit - tle sign: Shake me, I I
heart was long - ing for. Shake me, I

rat - tle. Squeeze me, I cry. As I
rat - tle. Squeeze me, I cry. I had
rat - tle. Squeeze me, I cry. As I

stood there be - side her I could hear her
count - ed my pen - nies, just a pen - ny
gave her the dol - ly that we both had longed to

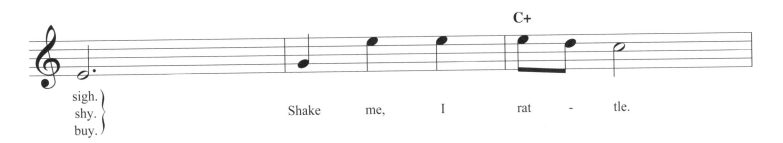

sigh.
shy.   Shake me, I rat - tle.
buy.

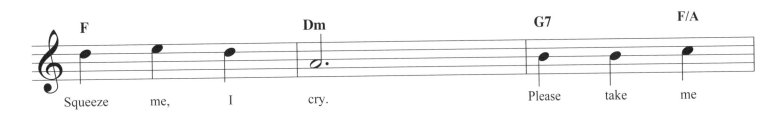

Squeeze me, I cry. Please take me

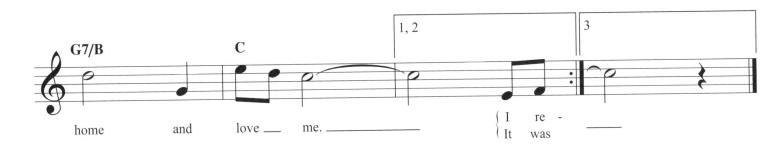

home and love ___ me. ___

I re - ___
It was

SILVER BELLS
from the Paramount Picture THE LEMON DROP KID

Words and Music by JAY LIVINGSTON
and RAY EVANS

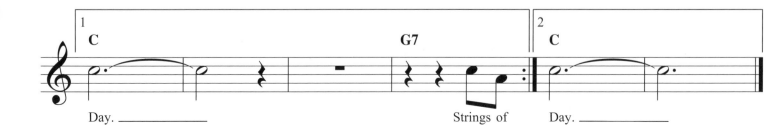

SNOWFALL

Lyrics by RUTH THORNHILL
Music by CLAUDE THORNHILL

SLEIGH RIDE

Music by LEROY ANDERSON
Words by MITCHELL PARISH

Moderately, in 2

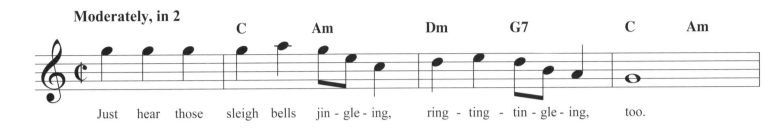

Just hear those sleigh bells jin - gle - ing, ring - ting - tin - gle - ing, too.

Come on, it's love - ly weath - er for a sleigh ride to - geth - er with you.

Out - side the snow is fall - ing and friends are call - ing, "Yoo hoo."

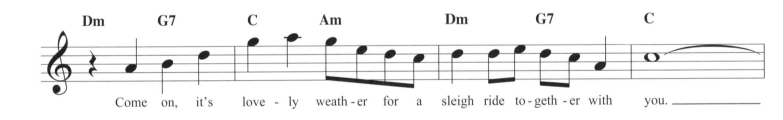

Come on, it's love - ly weath - er for a sleigh ride to - geth - er with you. _____

_____ Gid - dy - yap, gid - dy - yap, gid - dy - yap, let's go, let's look at the

show. We're rid - ing in a won - der - land of snow. _____

Gid - dy - yap, gid - dy - yap, gid - dy - yap, it's grand,

just hold - ing your hand. We're glid - ing a -

long with a song of a win - ter - y fair - y - land. Our cheeks are

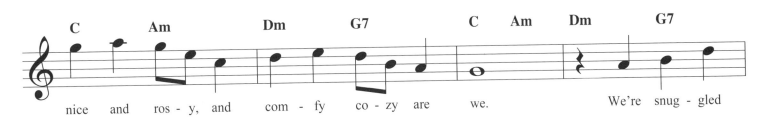

nice and ros - y, and com - fy co - zy are we. We're snug - gled

up to - geth - er like two birds of a feath - er would be. Let's take that

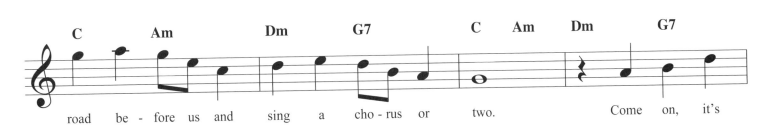

road be - fore us and sing a cho - rus or two. Come on, it's

love - ly weath - er for a sleigh ride to - geth - er with you.

SOME CHILDREN SEE HIM

Lyric by WIHLA HUTSON
Music by ALFRED BURT

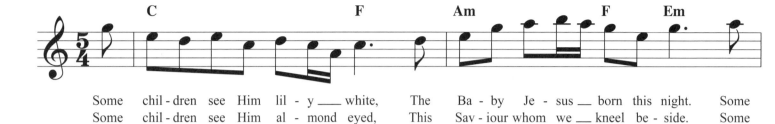

Some chil-dren see Him lil-y ___ white, The Ba - by Je - sus ___ born this night. Some
Some chil-dren see Him al - mond eyed, This Sav-iour whom we ___ kneel be - side. Some
The chil-dren in each dif - f'rent place Will see the Ba - by ___ Je - sus' face Like

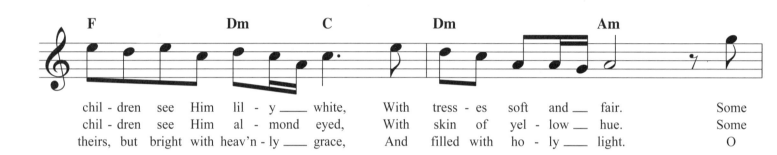

chil-dren see Him lil-y ___ white, With tress - es soft and ___ fair. Some
chil-dren see Him al - mond eyed, With skin of yel - low ___ hue. Some
theirs, but bright with heav'n - ly ___ grace, And filled with ho - ly ___ light. O

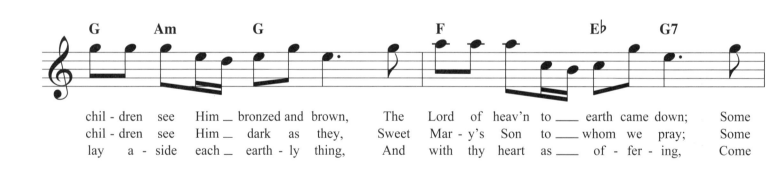

chil-dren see Him ___ bronzed and brown, The Lord of heav'n to ___ earth came down; Some
chil-dren see Him ___ dark as they, Sweet Mar - y's Son to ___ whom we pray; Some
lay a - side each ___ earth - ly thing, And with thy heart as ___ of - fer - ing, Come

chil-dren see Him bronzed and ___ brown, With dark and heav - y ___ hair.
chil-dren see Him dark as ___ they, And ah! they love him ___ too!
wor - ship now the In - fant ___ King, 'Tis love that's born to - night!

SOMEWHERE IN MY MEMORY
from the Twentieth Century Fox Motion Picture HOME ALONE

Words by LESLIE BRICUSSE
Music by JOHN WILLIAMS

Gently and with simplicity

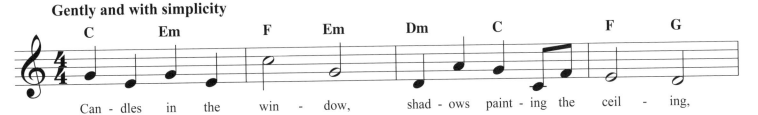

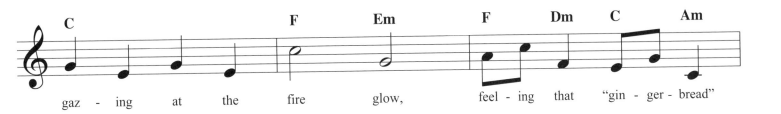

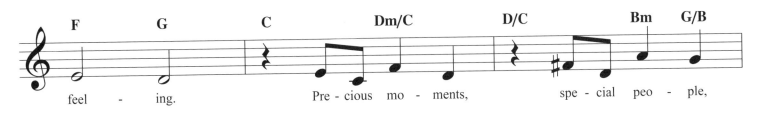

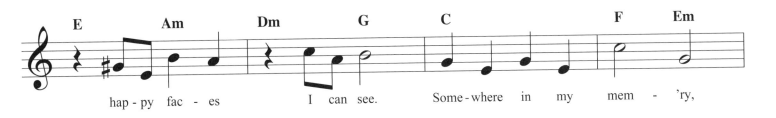

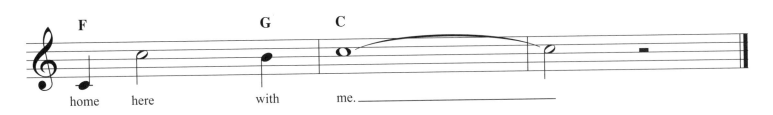

THE STAR CAROL

Lyric by WIHLA HUTSON
Music by ALFRED BURT

Tenderly, with much expression

Long years a - go on a deep __ win - ter night,
Je - sus, the Lord was that ba - by so small,
Dear Ba - by Je - sus, how ti - ny Thou art,

high in the heav'ns a ____ star ____ shone bright.
laid down to sleep in a hum - ble stall.
I'll make a place for ____ Thee __ in my heart.

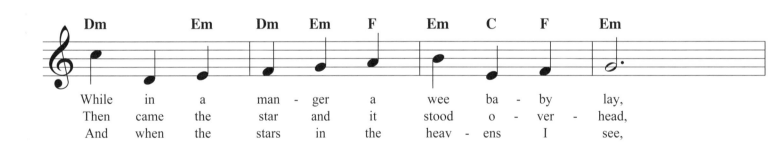

While in a man - ger a wee ba - by lay,
Then came the star and it stood o - ver - head,
And when the stars in the heav - ens I see,

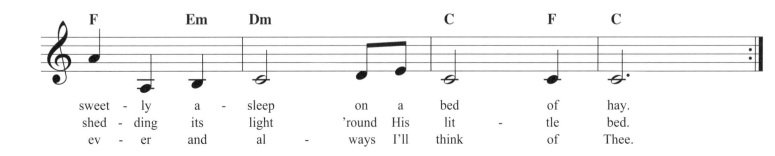

sweet - ly a - sleep on a bed of hay.
shed - ding its light 'round His lit - tle bed.
ev - er and al - ways I'll think of Thee.

SUZY SNOWFLAKE

Words and Music by SID TEPPER
and ROY BENNETT

THAT CHRISTMAS FEELING

Words and Music by BENNIE BENJAMIN
and GEORGE DAVID WEISS

THAT'S CHRISTMAS TO ME

Words and Music by KEVIN OLUSOLA
and SCOTT HOYING

Moderately

The fire - place is burn - ing bright, __ shin - ing all __ on me; I
see the chil - dren play out - side __ like an - gels in __ the snow, while

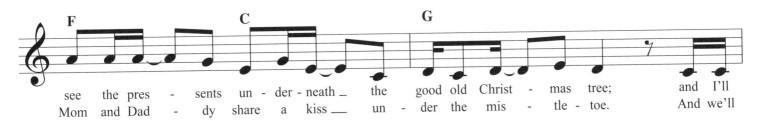

see the pres - sents un - der - neath __ the good old Christ - mas tree; and I'll
Mom and Dad - dy share a kiss __ un - der the mis - tle - toe. And we'll

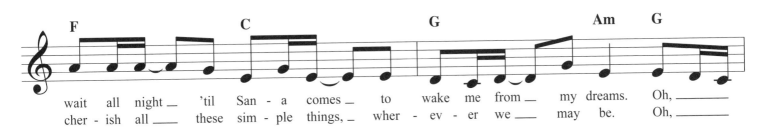

wait all night __ 'til San - a comes __ to wake me from __ my dreams. Oh, __
cher - ish all __ these sim - ple things, __ wher - ev - er we __ may be. Oh, __

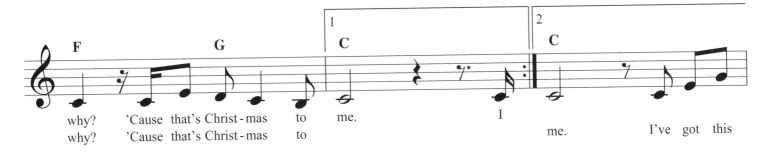

why? 'Cause that's Christ - mas to me.
why? 'Cause that's Christ - mas to me. I've got this

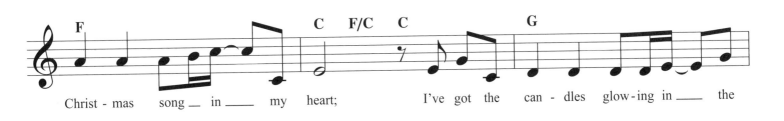

Christ - mas song __ in __ my heart; I've got the can - dles glow - ing in __ the

dark; __ I'm hang - ing all the stock - ings by the Christ - mas tree. __ Oh, __

THIS CHRISTMAS

Words and Music by DONNY HATHAWAY
and NADINE McKINNOR

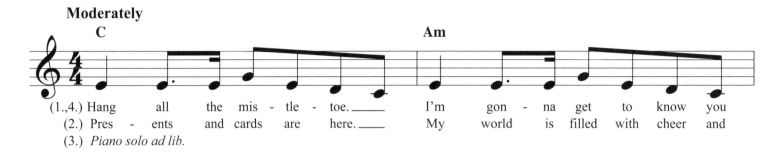

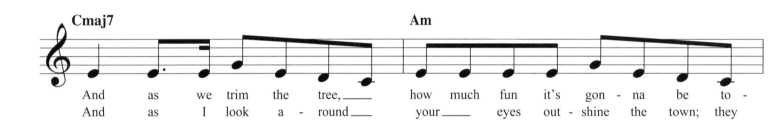

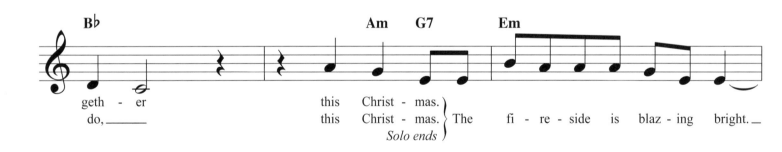

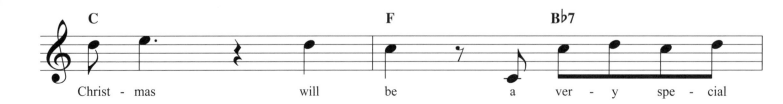

WE NEED A LITTLE CHRISTMAS
from MAME

Music and Lyric by
JERRY HERMAN

Brightly (as a polka)

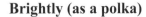

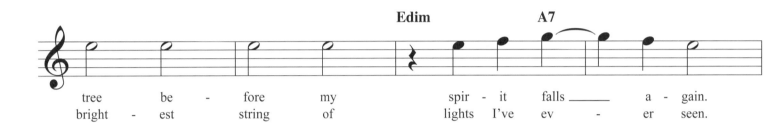
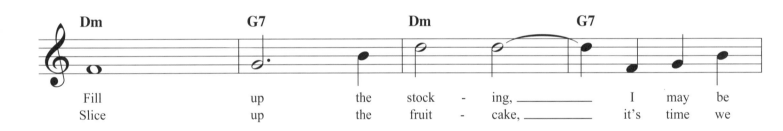
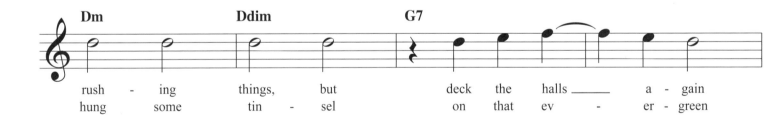
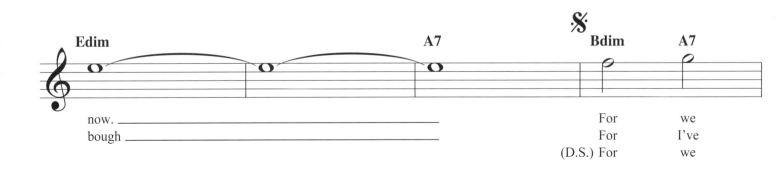

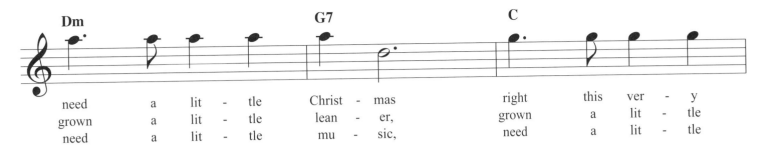

need a lit - tle Christ - mas right this ver - y
grown a lit - tle lean - er, grown a lit - tle
need a lit - tle mu - sic, need a lit - tle

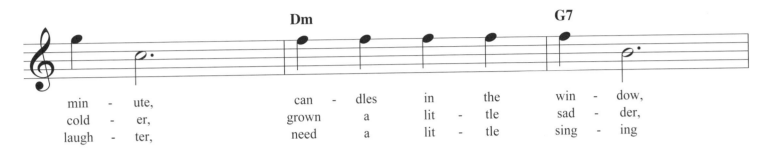

min - ute, can - dles in the win - dow,
cold - er, grown a lit - tle sad - der,
laugh - ter, need a lit - tle sing - ing

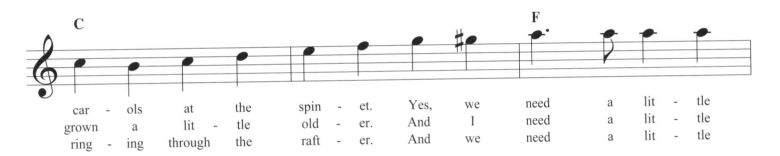

car - ols at the spin - et. Yes, we need a lit - tle
grown a lit - tle old - er. And I need a lit - tle
ring - ing through the raft - er. And we need a lit - tle

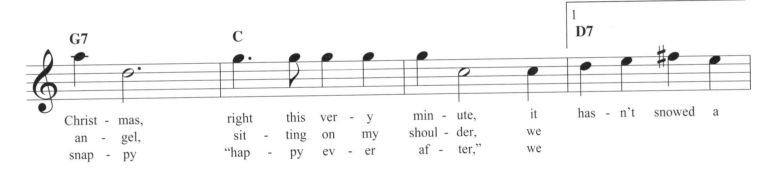

Christ - mas, right this ver - y min - ute, it has - n't snowed a
an - gel, sit - ting on my shoul - der, we
snap - py "hap - py ev - er af - ter," we

sin - gle flur - ry, but San - ta, dear, we're in a hur - ry. So

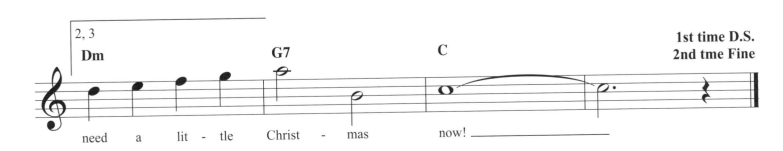

1st time D.S.
2nd tme Fine

need a lit - tle Christ - mas now!

WE WISH YOU THE MERRIEST

Words and Music by
LES BROWN

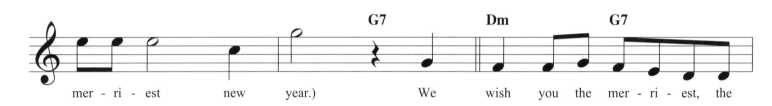

(We wish you the mer-ri-est, the mer-ri-est, the mer-ri-est, the mer-ri-est new year.) We wish you the mer-ri-est, the mer-ri-est, the mer-ri-est, yes, the mer-ri-est. We wish you the mer-ri-est, the mer-ri-est, the mer-ri-est yule cheer. We wish you the hap-pi-est, the hap-pi-est, the hap-pi-est, yes, the hap-pi-est. We wish you the hap-pi-est, the hap-pi-est, the hap-pi-est new year. May your

tree be filled with hap - pi - ness, hap - pi - ness and friend - li - ness for

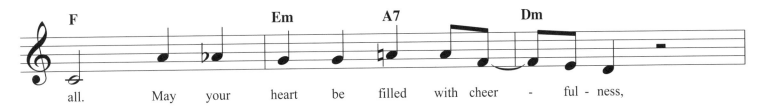

all. May your heart be filled with cheer - ful - ness,

hap - pi - ness and cheer - ful - ness for all. We wish you the hap - pi - est, the

hap - pi - est, hap - pi - est, yes, the hap - pi - est. We

wish you the mer - ri - est, the mer - ri - est, the mer - ri - est yule

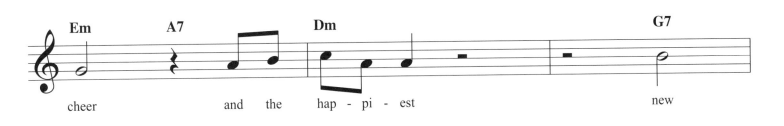

cheer and the hap - pi - est new

year. (We wish you the mer - ri - est, the

mer - ri - est,   the   mer - ri - est,   yes, the mer - ri - est.   We

wish   you the mer - ri - est, the mer - ri - est,   the   mer - ri - est   yule

cheer.)   We   wish   you the hap - pi - est, the hap - pi - est,   the

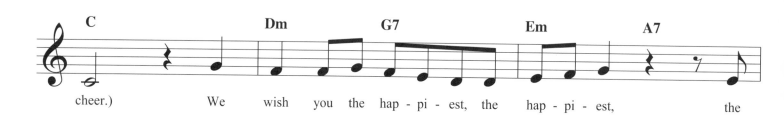

hap - pi - est,   yes, the hap - pi - est.   We   wish   you the hap - pi - est, the

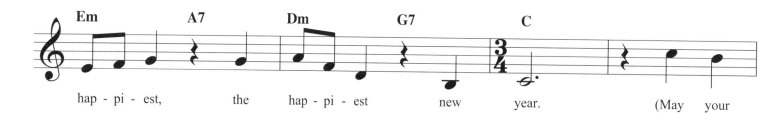

hap - pi - est,   the hap - pi - est   new   year.   (May your

tree   be   filled   with   hap - pi - ness,) _____

hap - pi - ness   and   friend - li - ness for   all.   (May your

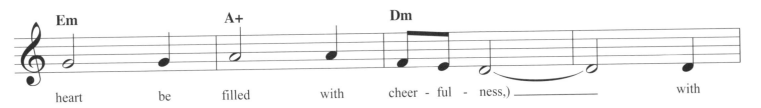

heart be filled with cheer - ful - ness,) _____ with

hap - pi - ness and cheer - ful - ness and friend - li - ness for all. We

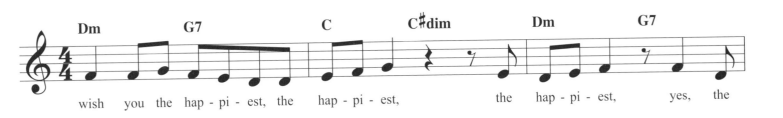

wish you the hap - pi - est, the hap - pi - est, the hap - pi - est, yes, the

hap - pi - est. We wish you the mer - ri - est, the mer - ri - est, the

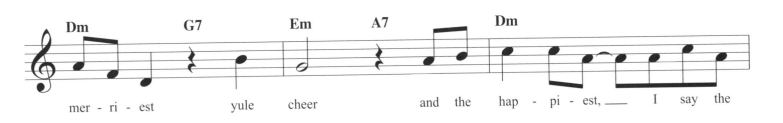

mer - ri - est yule cheer and the hap - pi - est, ___ I say the

friend - li - est ___ and the cheer - i - est, ___ and e - ven mer - ri - est new

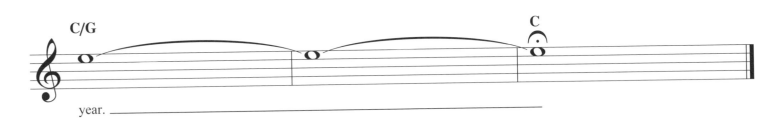

year. _____

WHAT ARE YOU DOING NEW YEAR'S EVE?

By FRANK LOESSER

Slowly and sentimentally

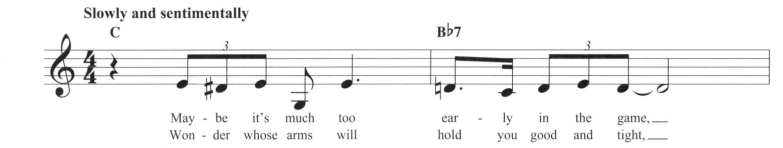

May - be it's much too ear - ly in the game, ___
Won - der whose arms will hold you good and tight, ___

ah, but I thought I'd ask you just the same. ___
when it's ex - act - ly twelve 'o - clock that night. ___

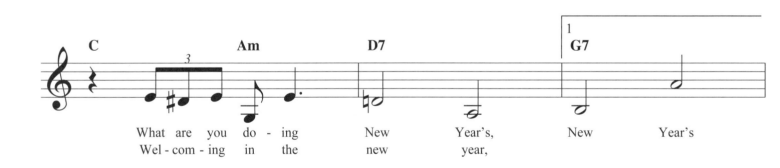

What are you do - ing the New Year's, New Year's
Wel - com - ing in the new year,

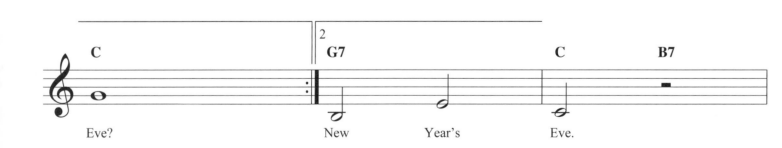

Eve? New Year's Eve.

May - be I'm cra - zy to sup - pose

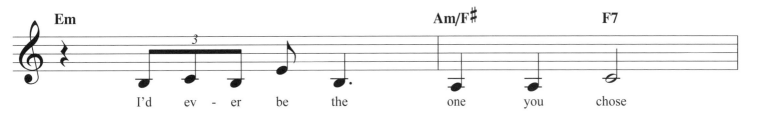

I'd ev - er be the one you chose

out of the thou - sand in - vi - ta - tions

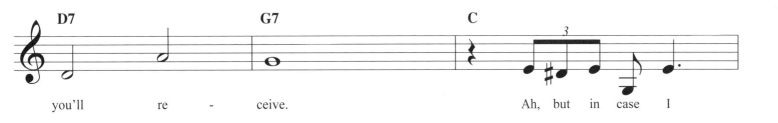

you'll re - ceive. Ah, but in case I

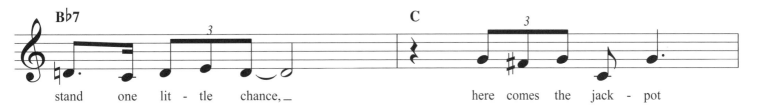

stand one lit - tle chance, here comes the jack - pot

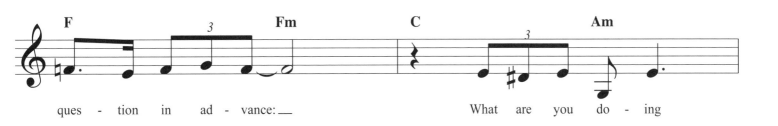

ques - tion in ad - vance: What are you do - ing

New Year's, New Year's Eve?

WHERE ARE YOU CHRISTMAS?
from DR. SEUSS' HOW THE GRINCH STOLE CHRISTMAS

Words and Music by WILL JENNINGS,
JAMES HORNER and MARIAH CAREY

181

WONDERFUL CHRISTMASTIME

Words and Music by
PAUL McCARTNEY

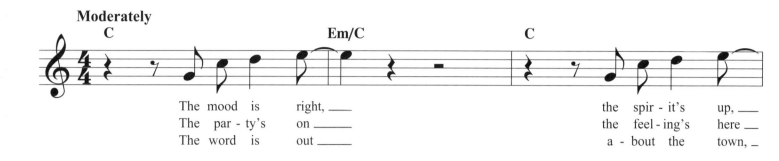

The mood is right, ___ the spir - it's up, ___
The par - ty's on ___ the feel - ing's here ___
The word is out ___ a - bout the town, ___

___ we're here to - night ___ and that's e - nough. _
___ that on - ly comes ___ this time of year. _
___ to lift a glass, ___ oh don't look down. _

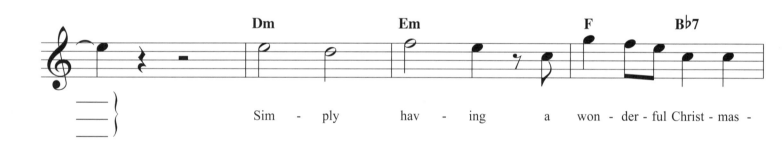

Sim - ply hav - ing a won - der - ful Christ - mas -

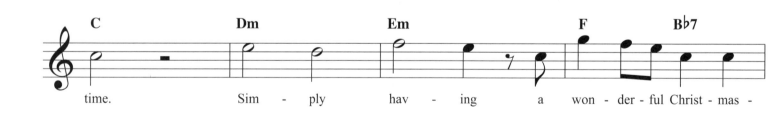

time. Sim - ply hav - ing a won - der - ful Christ - mas -

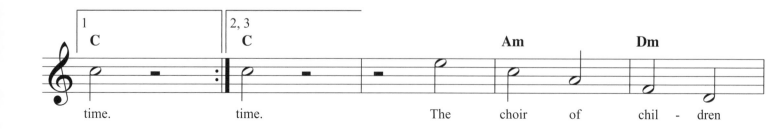

time. time. The choir of chil - dren

To Coda ⊕

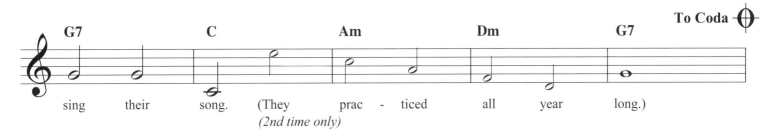

G7 **C** **Am** **Dm** **G7**

sing their song. (They prac - ticed all year long.)
(2nd time only)

C **F**

Ding dong, ding dong. Ding dong, ding. Ooh _____

Dm **F/C** **F**

_____ Ooh _____

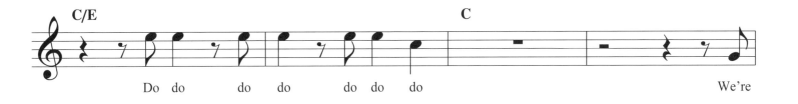

C/E **C**

Do do do do do do do We're

Dm **Em** **F** **B♭7** **C**

sim - ply hav - ing a won - der - ful Christ - mas - time.

Dm **Em** **F** **B♭7** **C** **D.C. al Coda**

Sim - ply hav - ing a won - der - ful Christ - mas - time.

CODA

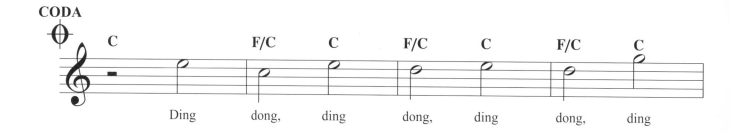

Ding dong, ding dong, ding dong, ding

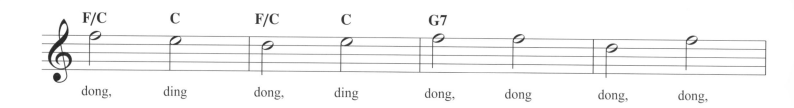

dong, ding dong, ding dong, dong dong, dong,

dong. The par - ty's on, _____ the spir - it's up, _

_____ we're here to - night _____

and that's e - nough. _ Sim - ply hav - ing a
sim - ply hav - ing a

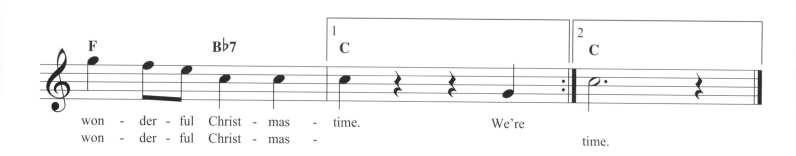

won - der - ful Christ - mas - time. We're
won - der - ful Christ - mas - time.

WHITE CHRISTMAS
from the Motion Picture Irving Berlin's HOLIDAY INN

Words and Music by
IRVING BERLIN

WINTER WONDERLAND

Words by DICK SMITH
Music by FELIX BERNARD

Sleigh - bells ring; are you lis - t'nin'? In the

lane, snow is glis - t'nin'. A beau - ti - ful sight, __ we're

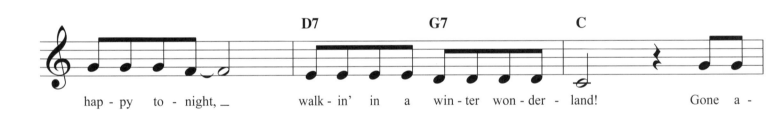

hap - py to - night, __ walk - in' in a win - ter won - der - land! Gone a -

way is the blue - bird, here to stay is a

new bird. { He sings a love song __ } { He's sing - ing a song __ } as we go a - long, __

walk - in' in a win - ter won - der - land! In the mead - ow we can build a

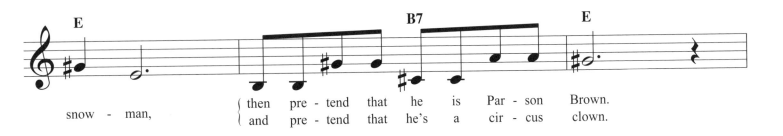

snow - man, { then pre - tend that he is Par - son Brown.
and pre - tend that he's a cir - cus clown. }

He'll say, "Are you mar - ried?" We'll say, "No, man! But you can do the job when you're in
We'll have lots of fun with Mis - ter Snow - man, un - til the oth - er kid - dies knock him

town!" Lat - er on, we'll con - spire ___ as we dream by the
down! When it snows, ain't it thrill - in', tho' your nose gets a

fire, ___ to face un - a - fraid ___ the plans that we made, ___ }
chill - in'? We'll frol - ic and play ___ the Es - ki - mo way, ___ }

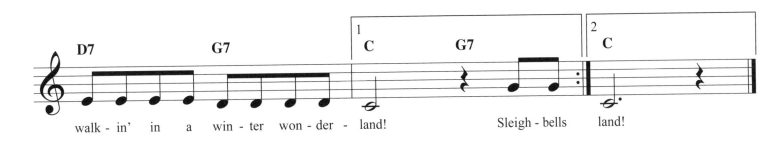

walk - in' in a win - ter won - der - land! Sleigh - bells land!

YOU'RE A MEAN ONE, MR. GRINCH

Lyrics by DR. SEUSS
Music by ALBERT HAGUE

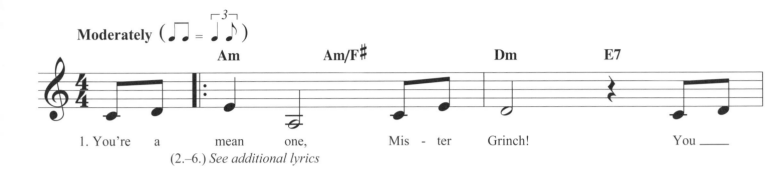

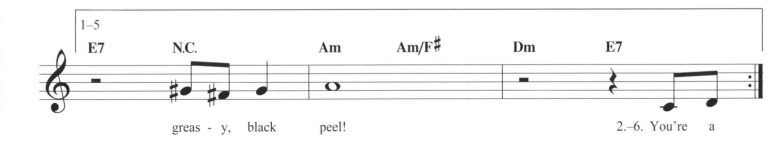

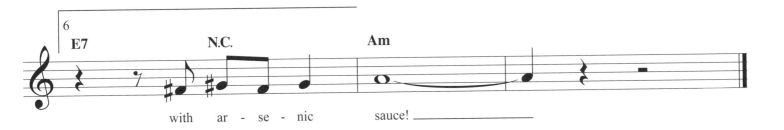

with ar - se - nic sauce! _____

Additional Lyrics

2. You're a monster, Mr. Grinch!
   Your heart's an empty hole.
   Your brain is full of spiders,
   You've got garlic in your soul, Mr. Grinch!
   I wouldn't touch you with a
   Thirty-nine-and-a-half-foot pole!

3. You're a vile one, Mr. Grinch!
   You have termites in your smile.
   You have all the tender sweetness
   Of a seasick crocodile, Mr. Grinch!
   *(Spoken:) Given the choice between the two of you,
      I'd take the...*
   (Sung:) seasick crocodile!

4. You're a foul one, Mr. Grinch!
   You're a nasty-wasty skunk!
   Your heart is full of unwashed socks,
   Your soul is full of gunk, Mr. Grinch!
   *(Spoken:) The three words that best describe you
      are as follows, and I quote:*
   (Sung:) Stink! Stank! Stunk!

5. You're a rotter, Mr. Grinch!
   You're the king of sinful sots.
   Your heart's a dead tomato
   Splotched with moldy, purple spots, Mr. Grinch!
   *(Spoken:) Your soul is an appalling dumpheap
      overflowing with the most disgraceful assortment of
      deplorable rubbish imaginable, mangled up in...*
   (Sung:) tangled-up knots!

6. You nauseate me, Mr. Grinch!
   With a nauseous, super "naus."
   You're a crooked jerkey jockey
   And you drive a crooked hoss, Mr. Grinch!
   *(Spoken:) You're a three-decker sauerkraut
      and toadstool sandwich...*
   (Sung:) with arsenic sauce!

YOU'RE ALL I WANT FOR CHRISTMAS

Words and Music by GLEN MOORE
and SEGER ELLIS

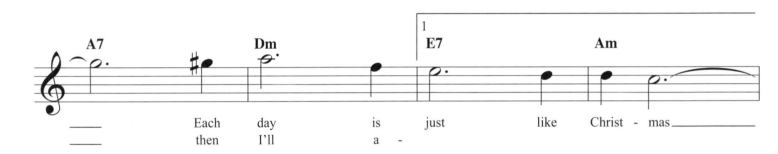

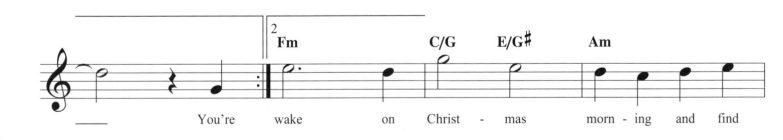

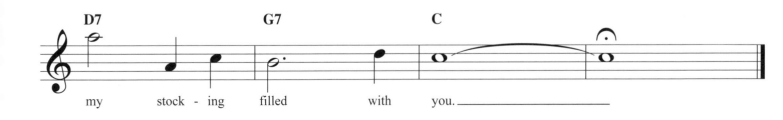

CHORD SPELLER

C chords

C	C–E–G
Cm	C–E♭–G
C7	C–E–G–B♭
Cdim	C–E♭–G♭
C+	C–E–G♯

C♯ or D♭ chords

C♯	C♯–F–G♯
C♯m	C♯–E–G♯
C♯7	C♯–F–G♯–B
C♯dim	C♯–E–G
C♯+	C♯–F–A

D chords

D	D–F♯–A
Dm	D–F–A
D7	D–F♯–A–C
Ddim	D–F–A♭
D+	D–F♯–A♯

E♭ chords

E♭	E♭–G–B♭
E♭m	E♭–G♭–B♭
E♭7	E♭–G–B♭–D♭
E♭dim	E♭–G♭–A
E♭+	E♭–G–B

E chords

E	E–G♯–B
Em	E–G–B
E7	E–G♯–B–D
Edim	E–G–B♭
E+	E–G♯–C

F chords

F	F–A–C
Fm	F–A♭–C
F7	F–A–C–E♭
Fdim	F–A♭–B
F+	F–A–C♯

F♯ or G♭ chords

F♯	F♯–A♯–C♯
F♯m	F♯–A–C♯
F♯7	F♯–A♯–C♯–E
F♯dim	F♯–A–C
F♯+	F♯–A♯–D

G chords

G	G–B–D
Gm	G–B♭–D
G7	G–B–D–F
Gdim	G–B♭–D♭
G+	G–B–D♯

G♯ or A♭ chords

A♭	A♭–C–E♭
A♭m	A♭–B–E♭
A♭7	A♭–C–E♭–G♭
A♭dim	A♭–B–D
A♭+	A♭–C–E

A chords

A	A–C♯–E
Am	A–C–E
A7	A–C♯–E–G
Adim	A–C–E♭
A+	A–C♯–F

B♭ chords

B♭	B♭–D–F
B♭m	B♭–D♭–F
B♭7	B♭–D–F–A♭
B♭dim	B♭–D♭–E
B♭+	B♭–D–F♯

B chords

B	B–D♯–F♯
Bm	B–D–F♯
B7	B–D♯–F♯–A
Bdim	B–D–F
B+	B–D♯–G

Important Note: A slash chord (C/E, G/B) tells you that a certain bass note is to be played under a particular harmony. In the case of C/E, the chord is C and the bass note is E.

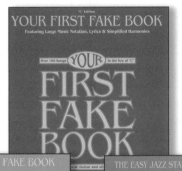

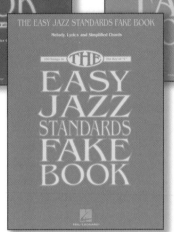
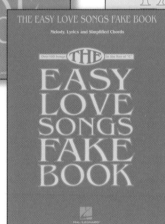
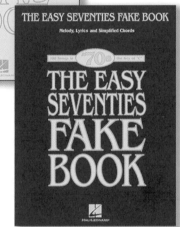